Building Web, Cloud, and Mobile Solutions with F#

Daniel Mohl

Beijing · Cambridge · Farnham · Köln · Sebastopol · Tokyo

Building Web, Cloud, and Mobile Solutions with F#

by Daniel Mohl

Copyright © 2013 Daniel Mohl. All rights reserved.

Printed in the United States of America.

Published by O'Reilly Media, Inc., 1005 Gravenstein Highway North, Sebastopol, CA 95472.

O'Reilly books may be purchased for educational, business, or sales promotional use. Online editions are also available for most titles (*http://my.safaribooksonline.com*). For more information, contact our corporate/institutional sales department: 800-998-9938 or *corporate@oreilly.com*.

Editor: Rachel Roumeliotis
Production Editor: Kara Ebrahim
Copyeditor: Audrey Doyle

Proofreader: Kara Ebrahim
Indexer: Ellen Troutman-Zaig
Cover Designer: Karen Montgomery
Interior Designer: David Futato
Illustrator: Rebecca Demarest

December 2012:   First Edition

Revision History for the First Edition:

2012-11-16   First release

See *http://oreilly.com/catalog/errata.csp?isbn=9781449333768* for release details.

ISBN: 978-1-449-33376-8

[LSI]

Table of Contents

Preface

If you were to do a search right now for the hottest technology trends, you would see a consistent theme of focus on the technical areas of web, cloud, and mobile solutions combined with big data and economies of scale. With these trends comes a need for tools that allow technologists, such as you and me, to harness these technical focal areas and bend them to our will. How do we achieve this? What combination of architectures, tools, languages, and techniques will make it possible for us to write programs that target multiple devices and scale effortlessly, while still allowing the solutions to be robust, maintainable, testable, and reusable?

A number of tools are available that meet many of our needs, but using them to their fullest potential while achieving our development goals requires more capabilities than they provide. To get the most bang for our buck we really need a language that is specifically intended to solve the challenges that these trends create. This language needs to inherently tackle complexities such as concurrency, asynchrony, and big data, while being able to seamlessly integrate with other languages, technologies, and tools that are best suited to resolve other challenges. Luckily for us this language exists today, and its name is F#.

In this book I will show you how to use F# to build key aspects of web, cloud, and mobile solutions to conquer these challenges. The expressive, powerful, succinct, and functional-first nature of F#, combined with technologies with which you are already familiar, such as ASP.NET MVC, ASP.NET Web API, WCF, Windows Azure, HTML5, CSS3, JavaScript, jQuery, and jQuery Mobile, will allow you to build incredible solutions that not only meet but exceed the demands of these current and future technology trends.

Who This Book Is For

This book is intended for technologists with experience in .NET who have heard about the benefits of F#, have at least a cursory understanding of the basic syntax, and wish to learn how to combine F# with other technologies to build better web, cloud, and mobile solutions. If you are brand new to F#, I encourage you to check out one of the many great F# books that provide information on getting started with F#, such as Chris Smith's *Programming F#, 3.0* (O'Reilly). If you are new to other platforms and frameworks mentioned in this book, such as ASP.NET MVC, WCF, ASP.NET Web API, Windows Azure, HTML, CSS, and/or jQuery Mobile, there are a number of other books offered by O'Reilly and other publishers that can quickly get you the information you need.

Getting Set Up to Run the Examples

The majority of the examples within this book were created with Visual Studio 2012. It is recommended that you use Visual Studio 2012 Professional or higher to run the examples; however, most of the examples will also work as expected with F# Tools for Visual Studio Express 2012 for Web, which was announced September 12, 2012, on the F# team blog (*http://bit.ly/fsharp-blog*). You can download F# Tools for Visual Studio Express 2012 for Web via the Microsoft Web Platform Installer here (*http://www.micro soft.com/web/gallery/install.aspx?appid=FSharpVWD11*). Depending on the platform or framework that is being targeted, installation of the following is required:

- ASP.NET MVC 4, which you can download and install here (*http://asp.net/mvc/ mvc4*).
- Windows Azure SDK and Developer Tools, which you can download and install here (*http://www.windowsazure.com/en-us/develop/net/*).

Additional installations and/or tools are referenced (when applicable) in the appropriate chapters.

How This Book Is Organized

This book provides everything you need to know to start building web, cloud, and mobile solutions with F#. In addition, it explores many of the latest technologies, platforms, and libraries such as Windows Azure, jQuery Mobile, SignalR, CouchDB, RavenDB, MongoDB, and more. The following provides a more detailed breakdown of what you will see in each chapter.

Chapter 1, Building an ASP.NET MVC 4 Web Application with F#

This chapter provides everything you need to get started building ASP.NET MVC 4 web applications with F# doing the majority of the server-side heavy lifting. Additionally, this chapter shows off several advanced techniques and F# language features that allow you to write more elegant code.

Chapter 2, Creating Web Services with F#

This chapter introduces the tools and concepts needed to create various types of web services including WCF SOAP and HTTP services, and approaches for interacting with a few of the available web micro-frameworks. The chapter also provides information on tools and techniques that are useful for unit-testing these services.

Chapter 3, To the Cloud! Taking Advantage of Azure

This chapter walks you through the creation of F# web applications and web services that run on Windows Azure. Additionally, it provides F# examples for interacting with several of the Azure APIs. Lastly, it talks about a few excellent examples of libraries and runtimes that have been built with F# to run on Azure.

Chapter 4, Constructing Scalable Web and Mobile Solutions

This chapter goes into more detail on how to use F# with other technologies to create scalable solutions that allow reuse by mobile and web frontends. The chapter includes information and/or examples for building web sockets, using SignalR, storing data in various NoSQL databases, and more.

Chapter 5, Functional Frontend Development

This chapter introduces LiveScript, Pit, and WebSharper, which are tools that, among other things, allow the creation of client-side code with a functional style. These tools make it possible to create end-to-end web stacks using functional concepts. A list of advantages, information on how to get started, and examples are provided for each option.

This book also features several appendixes that provide information that can help you on your journey toward developing cutting-edge web, cloud, and mobile solutions, but that do not fall directly into the scope of the main concepts covered in the core chapters.

Appendix A, Useful Tools and Libraries

This appendix lists and briefly describes several tools that can make your life easier as a web, cloud, and mobile solution developer.

Appendix B, Useful Websites

This appendix provides a number of links to websites that offer information on F# as well as other tools and libraries that are mentioned in the book.

Appendix C, Client-Side Technologies That Go Well with F#

This appendix briefly explores a few technologies that complement F# web and mobile development.

Conventions Used in This Book

The following typographical conventions are used in this book:

Italic

> Indicates new terms, URLs, email addresses, filenames, and file extensions.

`Constant width`

> Used for program listings, as well as within paragraphs to refer to program elements such as variable or function names, databases, data types, environment variables, statements, and keywords.

`Constant width bold`

> Shows commands or other text that should be typed literally by the user.

`Constant width italic`

> Shows text that should be replaced with user-supplied values or by values determined by context.

 This icon signifies a tip, suggestion, or general note.

 This icon indicates a warning or caution.

Using Code Examples

This book is here to help you get your job done. In general, you may use the code in this book in your programs and documentation. You do not need to contact us for permission unless you're reproducing a significant portion of the code. For example, writing a program that uses several chunks of code from this book does not require permission. Selling or distributing a CD-ROM of examples from O'Reilly books does require permission. Answering a question by citing this book and quoting example code does not require permission. Incorporating a significant amount of example code from this book into your product's documentation does require permission.

We appreciate, but do not require, attribution. An attribution usually includes the title, author, publisher, and ISBN. For example: "*Building Web, Cloud, and Mobile Solutions with F#* by Daniel Mohl (O'Reilly). Copyright 2013 Daniel Mohl, 978-1-449-33376-8."

If you feel your use of code examples falls outside fair use or the permission given above, feel free to contact us at *permissions@oreilly.com*.

Safari® Books Online

 Safari Books Online (*www.safaribooksonline.com*) is an on-demand digital library that delivers expert content in both book and video form from the world's leading authors in technology and business.

Technology professionals, software developers, web designers, and business and creative professionals use Safari Books Online as their primary resource for research, problem solving, learning, and certification training.

Safari Books Online offers a range of product mixes and pricing programs for organizations, government agencies, and individuals. Subscribers have access to thousands of books, training videos, and prepublication manuscripts in one fully searchable database from publishers like O'Reilly Media, Prentice Hall Professional, Addison-Wesley Professional, Microsoft Press, Sams, Que, Peachpit Press, Focal Press, Cisco Press, John Wiley & Sons, Syngress, Morgan Kaufmann, IBM Redbooks, Packt, Adobe Press, FT Press, Apress, Manning, New Riders, McGraw-Hill, Jones & Bartlett, Course Technology, and dozens more. For more information about Safari Books Online, please visit us online.

How to Contact Us

Please address comments and questions concerning this book to the publisher:

O'Reilly Media, Inc.
1005 Gravenstein Highway North
Sebastopol, CA 95472
800-998-9938 (in the United States or Canada)
707-829-0515 (international or local)
707-829-0104 (fax)

We have a web page for this book, where we list errata, examples, and any additional information. You can access this page at *http://oreil.ly/building-web*.

To comment or ask technical questions about this book, send email to *bookquestions@oreilly.com*.

For more information about our books, courses, conferences, and news, see our website at *http://www.oreilly.com*.

Find us on Facebook: *http://facebook.com/oreilly*

Follow us on Twitter: *http://twitter.com/oreillymedia*

Watch us on YouTube: *http://www.youtube.com/oreillymedia*

Acknowledgments

First and foremost, I'd like to thank my wife (Melissa) and daughter (Eva) for putting up with me during the many hours of heads-down computer time that it took to bring this book to fruition.

I'd also like to thank the following people for their great work, support, guidance, and/ or awesomeness!

- Don Syme and the rest of the F# team
- Rachel Roumeliotis
- Elijah Manor
- Stephen Swensen
- Fahad Suhaib
- Ryan Riley
- Steffen Forkmann
- Anton Tayanovskyy
- Adam Granicz

CHAPTER 1

Building an ASP.NET MVC 4 Web Application with F#

> *Any sufficiently advanced technology is*
> *indistinguishable from magic.*
>
> —Sir Arthur Charles Clarke

I've always loved magic. For as long as I can remember, I have enjoyed watching master magicians performing their craft. As I grew up, I read every book I could find on how to master the tricks that astounded me through the years. I quickly found that I enjoyed learning how to perform magic tricks even more than I enjoyed watching them.

As Sir Arthur Charles Clarke states, technology can often feel like magic. Maybe that is why I love technology so much. F# falls into this category more so than many of the other languages I have used throughout my programming exploits. The features that it provides bring great power that can occasionally feel like magic. Sometimes it can be difficult to determine how best to apply that magic in practical ways to achieve better, faster, and more scalable web, cloud, and mobile solutions. This book will show you how to leverage the full power of F# to solve your everyday development problems.

In this chapter you will start your journey by exploring F# combined with ASP.NET MVC 4. You will learn how to quickly kick-start one of these projects, do some basic ASP.NET MVC development in F#, and apply a few of the more advanced F# features to improve the code you write. Additionally, several topics and techniques that are not specifically related to ASP.NET MVC 4, but are commonly used in conjunction with this framework, will be exemplified. Throughout the chapter, features of F# that may seem magical will be demystified.

The rest of the book will explore additional platforms, technologies, libraries, and features that you can use with F# to create cutting-edge web, cloud, and mobile solutions.

The F# ASP.NET MVC 4 Project Templates

The developer preview of ASP.NET MVC 4 was officially announced after the Build conference in the latter half of 2011. In February 2012, the beta release of ASP.NET MVC 4 was announced and the release candidate followed at the end of May 2012. Version 4 brought many new improvements and enhancements to the already full-featured ASP.NET MVC offering. To learn more about ASP.NET MVC 4, visit their website (*http://www.asp.net/mvc/mvc4*).

The most efficient way to use F# with ASP.NET MVC 4 is to take advantage of the inherent separation of concerns built into the MVC design pattern. You can then utilize the provided boundaries to leverage the strengths of the C# ecosystem and the F# language features, respectively. In the case of the ASP.NET MVC framework, this is accomplished by establishing a C# ASP.NET MVC project to house the views and all client-side concerns, while using an F# project for the models, controllers, and any other server-side concerns. Figure 1-1 shows the typical MVC pattern implemented in ASP.NET MVC with a designation of component to project type.

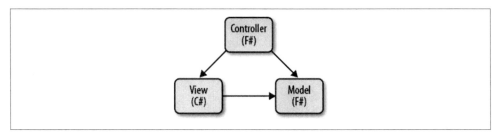

Figure 1-1. MVC pattern with project type designation

While you can manually create a boilerplate solution with the aforementioned project structure, the process will quickly become tedious. Additionally, these mundane setup steps cause an unnecessary barrier to entry to using F# in your ASP.NET MVC solutions. To help eliminate these issues, a project template (*http://bit.ly/fsharpmvc4projecttem plate*) has been created and made available through Visual Studio Gallery.

 If, for whatever reason, you are not running ASP.NET MVC 4, templates are also available for ASP.NET MVC 3 and ASP.NET MVC 2. A list of many of the available project templates can be found here (*http://bit.ly/ allfsprojecttemplates*).

Finding and Installing the Templates

Thanks to Visual Studio Gallery, finding and installing the ASP.NET MVC 4 F# project templates couldn't be easier. Simply launch the Project Creation Wizard through whichever method your prefer—my favorite is the Ctrl-Shift-N keyboard shortcut—select Online in the lefthand navigation pane, search for "fsharp mvc4" in the search box at the upper-right corner, select the "F# C# MVC 4" template, and click OK. Figure 1-2 shows an example of the Project Creation Wizard just before OK is to be clicked.

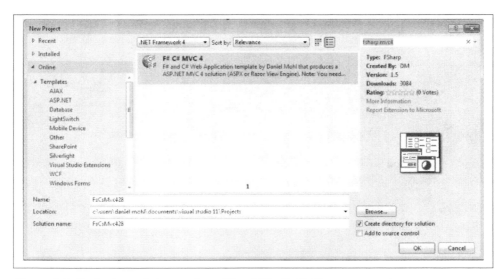

Figure 1-2. Project template search on Visual Studio Gallery

 While you could use the approach mentioned here every time you wish to create a new F# ASP.NET MVC 4 project, you really only have to do this once. After the initial installation, a new template will become available under the Installed category in the lefthand navigation pane. The template is named "F# and C# Web Application (ASP.NET MVC 4)" and you can access it by selecting Visual F#→ASPNET.

After you click OK, a dialog (shown in Figure 1-3) will display from which you can select the type of solution you want to generate and the view engine you want to use, as well as whether you want to include a project you can use to write unit tests. Once you make your selections and click OK, the projects are generated and the applicable NuGet packages are automatically installed. For many of the rest of the examples in this chapter, I will assume you selected the Razor view engine during this process.

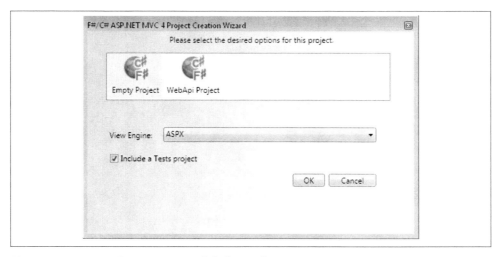

Figure 1-3. Project Creation Wizard dialog with F# ASP.NET MVC

Exploring the C# Project

If you have created any C#-only ASP.NET MVC projects, the C# solution should look very familiar to you. There are really only three primary differences:

1. There is no *Controllers* folder.
2. There is no *Models* folder.
3. The *Global.asax* file doesn't have a corresponding *Global.asax.cs* file.

The primary reason for these changes is that each has been pushed to the F# project that was generated along with this C# project. We'll look at this F# project in more detail in the next section. The *Global.asax* file is a little interesting in that it still requires some programmatic method for association to the F# class. The following code from the *Global.asax* markup shows how this is done:

```
<%@ Application Inherits="FsWeb.Global" Language="C#" %>
<script Language="C#" RunAt="server">

  // Defines the Application_Start method and calls Start in
  // System.Web.HttpApplication from which Global inherits.
  protected void Application_Start(Object sender, EventArgs e) {
      base.Start();
  }

</script>
```

Dissecting the F# Project

If you selected the "Empty Project" template on the Project Creation Wizard, then the resultant F# project is very simple. The project is generated with all necessary MVC assembly references and two *.fs* files: *Global.fs* and *HomeController.fs*. I already briefly mentioned the *Global.fs* file and I'm sure you can guess what *HomeController.fs* is. I'll review them in detail in this section.

Global.fs

As previously mentioned, the *Global.fs* file contains most of the code that would normally go into the *Global.asax.cs* file, but with a few F# twists. The first thing you may notice is the Route type. This is an *F# record type* that is being used to contain routing definitions. Record types are immutable by default. Because of this, they go very well with the highly concurrent and stateless nature of the Web. I'll talk more about uses for record types throughout this book. The Route record type is as follows:

```
type Route = { controller : string
               action : string
               id : UrlParameter }
```

 The Route type is only used for the standard controller/action/ID route. Custom types are needed to accommodate other routing patterns.

After declaring the Route type, a class named Global is defined, which inherits from System.Web.HttpApplication. The code within Global looks pretty similar to the C# equivalent, with the exception of the MapRoutes method call and the use of significant whitespace rather than braces to define scope. The main difference associated with the MapRoutes method call is directly related to the Route record. Instead of "newing up" an anonymous type to pass the route information to MapRoutes, F# type inference is being leveraged to create a new Route record. This record creation syntax is known as a *record expression*. The Global class is shown in the following example with the Route record creation code emphasized:

```
type Global() =
    inherit System.Web.HttpApplication()

    static member RegisterRoutes(routes:RouteCollection) =
        routes.IgnoreRoute("{resource}.axd/{*pathInfo}")
        routes.MapRoute("Default",
                        "{controller}/{action}/{id}",
                        { controller = "Home"; action = "Index"
                          id = UrlParameter.Optional } )
```

```
member this.Start() =
    AreaRegistration.RegisterAllAreas()
    Global.RegisterRoutes(RouteTable.Routes)
```

HomeController.fs

The *HomeController.fs* file contains the definition for the HomeController class. This class inherits from Controller and implements a single action named Index. We will explore controllers in more detail later in this chapter. Here are the contents of the *HomeController.fs* file:

```
namespace FsWeb.Controllers

open System.Web
open System.Web.Mvc

[<HandleError>]
type HomeController() =
    inherit Controller()
    member this.Index () =
        this.View() :> ActionResult
```

You may be curious about the :> symbol that is emphasized in the preceding example. This symbol indicates an *upcast* to type ActionResult of the result from this.View(). In this example, the cast to ActionResult isn't really necessary, but it would be required in certain circumstances, so the template adds the upcast for example purposes. If you were to instead explicitly specify the return type of the Index method like this:

```
member this.Index () : ActionResult = …
```

then the cast could have been written as:

```
upcast this.View()
```

Since the cast isn't really needed in this specific case, you can simply change this method to the following:

```
member this.Index () =
    this.View()
```

Type checking for an upcast occurs at compile time to ensure validity of the cast. A *downcast* (i.e., :?>), on the other hand, is only checked at runtime. If there is any chance that the downcast will fail, it is recommended that you use a type test in a match expression. You could also wrap the expression in a try/with statement, then catch the Invalid CastException, but this is less efficient than the type test approach.

F# Controllers and Models

Since the primary focus of this book is on how to use F# to best complement the larger technology stack, I will be spending a lot more time talking about controllers and models than views. F# provides several unique features that lend themselves well to the creation of various aspects of controllers and models. I'll show you a few of these in this section and cover more advanced features in later sections.

To help facilitate the discussion of controllers and models, I will walk you through the creation of a new page in the web application, paying special attention to the code used to create the model and controller. This new page will display a simple jQuery Mobile list view that is driven and populated by a new controller and model.

To kick things off, you need to create a new View. To do this, create a new folder under the *Views* folder named *Guitars* and add a new ASP.NET MVC view to the folder, named *Index*. Make sure to uncheck the "Use a layout or master page:" option in the ASP.NET MVC view item template wizard. You can now change the view markup to match the following:

```
@model IEnumerable<FsWeb.Models.Guitar>
<!DOCTYPE html>
<html>
<head>
    <title>@ViewBag.Title</title>
    <meta name="viewport" content="width=device-width, initial-scale=1" />
    <link rel="stylesheet"
        href="http://code.jquery.com/mobile/1.0.1/jquery.mobile-1.0.1.min.css" />
</head>

<body>
    <div data-role="page" data-theme="a" id="guitarsPage">
        <div data-role="header">
            <h1>Guitars</h1>
        </div>
        <div data-role="content">
        <ul data-role="listview" data-filter="true" data-inset="true">
            @foreach(var x in Model) {
                <li><a href="#">@x.Name</a></li>
            }
        </ul>
        </div>
    </div>
    <script src="http://code.jquery.com/jquery-1.6.4.min.js">
    </script>
    <script src="http://code.jquery.com/mobile/1.0.1/jquery.mobile-1.0.1.min.js">
    </script>

    <script>
        $(document).delegate("#guitarsPage", 'pageshow', function (event) {
            $("div:jqmData(role='content') > ul").listview('refresh');
```

```
        });
    </script>
</body>
</html>
```

 Since the focus of this section is not on the view, I've consolidated everything into a single *cshtml* file for the purpose of simplicity. In production code, you would want to create a separate module for the JavaScript code (and likely use something like RequireJS to help load and manage the JavaScript modules). Also, you would want to create a separate Layout page for reuse by all mobile pages. Additionally, ASP.NET MVC 4 includes a convention-based approach for mobile development that involves adding ".Mobile" or something more device-specific to the names of views. You can learn more about the best practices for view creation here (*http://www.asp.net/mvc/tutorials*).

Controllers

To create the basic controller for the new view, add a new F# source file to the F# project, name it *GuitarsController.fs*, and populate it with code that matches the following:

```
namespace FsWeb.Controllers

open System.Web.Mvc
open FsWeb.Models

[<HandleError>]
type GuitarsController() =
    inherit Controller()
    member this.Index () =
        // The sequence is hardcoded for example purposes only.
        // It will be switched out in a future example.
        seq { yield Guitar(Name = "Gibson Les Paul")
              yield Guitar(Name = "Martin D-28") }
        |> this.View
```

This looks very similar to the HomeController with the exception of the *sequence expression* and the *pipe-forward operator*. For this example, the sequence expression is providing a collection of Guitar model instances to be passed to the view. This "hardcoded" data will be replaced with a call to a repository in a future example.

The second point of interest is the use of the pipe-forward operator. In this example, the pipe-forward operator is being used to pipe the sequence of Guitar as the model argument for the overloaded method of View, which takes a single obj argument.

The obj keyword is an F#-type alias for object. I will talk more about type aliases in Chapter 2.

Models

Models can be created with either F# record types or classes. Out of the box, F# records work well for read-only data and allow the models to be slightly simpler. In F# 3.0, a new attribute called CLIMutable has been added that makes F# records an excellent option for read/write scenarios as well. I will talk more about the CLIMutable attribute in Chapter 4. Here is an example of a Guitar model built with an F# record:

```
namespace FsWeb.Models

type Guitar = { Id : Guid; Name : string }
```

 Prior to F# 3.0, F# record usage in both read-only and read/write situations was possible, but more difficult. This is because F# records do not have a parameterless constructor. The best solution to this problem (prior to F# 3.0) was to use a custom *model binder*.

The second option for building models with F# is to create the models as classes. The controller example that I showed in the preceding section assumes that the class approach is used. The code example that follows demonstrates how to build a Guitar model class in F# (this class, as well as most of the examples in this book, was written with F# 3.0; the syntax would be slightly different in F# 2.0 since auto-properties is a new feature in F# 3.0):

```
namespace FsWeb.Models

type Guitar() =
    member val Name = "" with get, set
```

You can also add any desired Data Annotations to the model class. The following adds the Required data annotation attribute to the Name property:

```
open System.ComponentModel.DataAnnotations

type Guitar() =
    [<Required>] member val Name = "" with get, set
```

 The Required attribute doesn't provide value in this example, but it will be useful for the many scenarios where changes are being made from the UI.

the model we will use for the Entity Framework example in the next section:

```
ace FsWeb.Models

open System
open System.ComponentModel.DataAnnotations

type Guitar() =
    [<Key>] member val Id = Guid.NewGuid() with get, set
    [<Required>] member val Name = "" with get, set
```

Interacting with a Database

If you were to run the web application right now you would see a simple screen that displays a collection of guitar names. However, it's still not very useful due to the data being hardcoded. Luckily, you have several choices when it comes to using F# to interact with a database for storage and/or retrieval of data.

Entity Framework

Entity Framework (EF) is probably the most common way to interact with an SQL Server database when working in ASP.NET MVC. Adoption is continuing to grow, especially now that EF supports a code-first approach. The F#/C# ASP.NET MVC 4 template already added all of the assembly references you need in order to start working with EF. With this done, you start using it by creating a class that inherits from `DbContext`. The following code shows an example of this:

```
namespace FsWeb.Repositories

open System.Data.Entity
open FsWeb.Models

type FsMvcAppEntities() =
    inherit DbContext("FsMvcAppExample")

    do Database.SetInitializer(new CreateDatabaseIfNotExists<FsMvcAppEntities>())

    [<DefaultValue()>] val mutable guitars : IDbSet<Guitar>
    member x.Guitars with get() = x.guitars and set v = x.guitars <- v
```

There isn't anything too crazy going on here. We're simply using some of the out-of-the-box EF API features, defining an `IDbSet` of guitars, and creating a `Guitars` property with both a getter and a setter.

You can learn more about the EF API here (*http://bit.ly/efcodefirstwalk through*).

Now you need to add a repository class to allow retrieval of all the guitars from the database.

The repository class isn't technically needed; however, it is considered by many to be a best practice and has become a standard in most applications.

Here's the code that shows the creation of a `GuitarsRepository` class:

```
namespace FsWeb.Repositories

type GuitarsRepository() =
    member x.GetAll () =
        use context = new FsMvcAppEntities()
        query { for g in context.Guitars do
                select g }
        |> Seq.toList
```

If you need to use EF in F# 2.0, the query syntax in the preceding example will not work (since it's new to F# 3.0). For F# 2.0, you can do similar things by installing the `FSPowerPack.Linq.Community` NuGet package, opening `Microsoft.FSharp.Linq.Query`, and changing the syntax to something similar to the code that follows:

```
query <@ seq { for g in context.Guitars -> g } @> |> Seq.toList
```

This functionality from the F# PowerPack uses a feature of F# called *quoted expressions*, which allows you to generate an abstract syntax tree (AST) and process and evaluate it as needed. While there are many uses for quoted expressions, one common use case is to generate F# code or code in other languages.

The first thing the `GetAll` method does is instantiate a `DbContext`. Notice how the `use` keyword takes the place of the standard `let` keyword. This ensures that the object will be disposed appropriately after use—it's similar to wrapping code in a `using` statement in C#, but doesn't require that you wrap any additional code.

The `GetAll` method then performs a query against the database. The *query* syntax used to accomplish this is a new feature in F# 3.0 that makes data manipulation a bit easier. While the syntax acts like it's a new compiler feature, it is actually an implementation of an F# feature called *computation expressions*. I'll show you an example of how to build your own custom computation expressions later in this chapter. In the next section, we'll explore the query computation expression in more detail.

With those two steps complete, all that is left to do is to switch out the hardcoded data that we originally added to the Index action in GuitarsController:

```
[<HandleError>]
type GuitarsController(repository : GuitarsRepository) =
    inherit Controller()
    new() = new GuitarsController(GuitarsRepository())
    member this.Index () =
        repository.GetAll()
        |> this.View
```

In some ways this change simplifies the code (especially the Index action), but it also adds a little complexity with the new overloaded constructor. This serves a few purposes:

- By allowing the repository to be passed into the constructor, it opens the door for the use of *Inversion of Control* (IoC) containers. For the sake of simplicity, the preceding example does not include all of the changes that would be necessary to make optimal use of an IoC container.

- It makes the controller more testable. By providing an overloaded constructor, you have the ability to pass in a fake repository class that allows the controller actions to be tested without requiring database interaction.

Since out-of-the-box ASP.NET MVC requires the controller to have a constructor that takes no parameters, you also have to include this line of code:

```
new() = new GuitarsController(GuitarsRepository())
```

This provides the needed constructor and then calls the main constructor with a new GuitarsRepository.

To wrap this up and try out your new database interaction, make sure the *web.config* in the C# Web Application project has an appropriately named connection string, such as:

```
<add name="FsMvcAppExample"
    connectionString="YOUR CONNECTION STRING"
    providerName="System.Data.SqlClient" />
```

You can now run the application to have EF automatically create the database and table. Add some records to the Guitars table and put on your party hat. An example of what the web page should look like when you go to *http://localhost:[port]/Guitars* is shown in Figure 1-4.

Figure 1-4. Guitar list with ASP.NET MVC 4 and jQuery Mobile

Querying the Data

The new query syntax that you saw in the preceding section looks and feels a bit like LINQ in C#/VB.NET. Here are a few more quick examples of how it can be used:

Get a guitar by name.

```
member x.GetByName name =
    use context = new FsMvcAppEntities()
    query { for g in context.Guitars do
            where (g.Name = name) }
    |> Seq.toList
```

Sort the guitars by name.

```
member x.GetAllAlphabetic () =
    use context = new FsMvcAppEntities()
    query { for g in context.Guitars do
            sortBy g.Name }
    |> Seq.toList
```

Get the top X records.

```
member x.GetTop rowCount =
    use context = new FsMvcAppEntities()
    query { for g in context.Guitars do
            take rowCount }
    |> Seq.toList
```

A number of additional examples are available here (*http://fsharp3sample.code plex.com/*).

You can also use many of the previous examples with the F# `PowerPack` `Linq` approach, though the syntax is not as clean.

Querying with Type Providers

F# 3.0 has another new feature called *type providers*, which makes interacting with the database even easier. To use a type provider to access the database, you first need to add a reference to `FSharp.Data.TypeProviders`. You can then use one of the database-related out-of-the-box type providers such as `SqlDataConnection`. This type of provider gets the database schema and generates appropriate types on the fly. Here's an example:

```
open Microsoft.FSharp.Data.TypeProviders

type DbConnection =
    SqlDataConnection<ConnectionStringName="FsMvcAppExample",
                      ConfigFile="web.config">

type GuitarsRepository2() =
    member x.GetAll () =
        use context = DbConnection.GetDataContext()
        query { for g in context.Guitars do
                select (Guitar(Id = g.Id, Name = g.Name)) }
        |> Seq.toList
```

An extra step is needed to get IntelliSense for `context` inside the F# WebApp project. To accomplish this, simply create a *web.config* file in the F# WebApp project and add appropriate database connection string elements.

Once this is done, you can query the results with the same query syntax I showed you in "Entity Framework" (page 10). This may not seem all that different from the previous Entity Framework approach, but the great thing here is that the `FsMvcAppEntities` type is not needed and can be completely eliminated. Additionally, the `Guitar` model class is now simpler as the [`<Key>`] attribute is no longer needed.

Going into extensive detail about how type providers work is beyond the scope of this book, but at a high level the following is occurring:

1. A magic fairy generates pixie dust that swirls and twirls into your computer.

2. By using the query computation expression you can now interact with the database.

If you want to learn about the "real" inner workings of type providers, I suggest checking out the documentation for creating type providers on MSDN (*http://bit.ly/creatingtypeproviders*). Additionally, I have created a sample custom type provider on my blog (*http://bit.ly/dmohlty peproviderexample*). Note that I created the example from my blog with the developer preview of F# 3.0. It is likely that things have changed since then.

Luckily for us, the specifics of how this stuff works aren't all that important. All you need to know is the simple syntax you just learned. The out-of-the-box SQL-related type providers are packed with a number of benefits as long as the database you're interacting with already exists. However, the rest of the examples in this chapter take a code-first approach. Because of this, I will use the previously shown Entity Framework approach for these examples. In Chapter 2, I will show an example that uses the type provider approach.

Taking Advantage of F#

You now have the tools and techniques you need in order to build a simple web app with F# and C# ASP.NET MVC 4. You've also seen a few of the great features that F# has to offer to help you on your journey, such as record types, sequence expressions, the pipe-forward operator, and one of the out-of-the-box computation expressions. However, this barely scratches the surface of what F# can do for you. The next few sections will provide several more "magical" F# features that will help you on your way.

The first thing you may have noticed in the examples thus far is that we are still building the ASP.NET MVC code using a mostly object-oriented approach. This is all well and good, and you can certainly use this approach to build solid web solutions that accomplish the majority of your goals; however, there are several advantages that you can gain by moving to a more functional paradigm.

Moving to a More Functional Approach

You may have noticed a couple of things about the guitar controller and repository. The repository has a separate class that designates a `GuitarRepository`. If a new repository is required in the future, to retrieve something like trumpets, you would likely have to create a very similar repository class called `TrumpetRepository`. Having to do this often will result in a lot of code that breaks the *Don't Repeat Yourself* (DRY) best practice. One way to solve this using a functional paradigm is to create a generic module with reusable functions that take other functions as arguments. Functions that take or return other functions are known as *higher-order functions*. The following shows an example:

```
namespace FsWeb.Repositories

open System
open System.Linq

module Repository =
    let get (source:IQueryable<_>) queryFn =
        queryFn source |> Seq.toList

    let getAll () =
        fun s -> query { for x in s do
                            select x }
```

This code defines a `Repository` module—which provides a named grouping of F# constructs such as functions. The functions in the `Repository` module are fairly generic and reusable due to F#'s support of functions as a first-class citizen. The `get` function takes two arguments:

- An object named `source` that must be of type `IQueryable<_>`.
- A function that takes `source` as an argument. This function, which could be anything that takes `source` as the last argument and that can then be passed into `Seq.toList` after the function is evaluated, will execute the query computation expression.

 The `Repository` module is similar in concept to the generic repository pattern in C# that uses `IRepository<T>` and/or `Repository<T>`. While some consider this to be an unnecessary abstraction layer, I feel this approach improves readability and reduces code duplication. Although several of the examples in this book use a generic repository approach, the query computation expression can certainly be used without the additional abstraction.

With the `get` function defined, we can create any number of additional query functions that can be passed into `get` as the second argument. The `getAll` function in the example shows how to do this. Other examples include the following:

```
let find filterPredFn =
    filterPredFn
    |> fun fn s -> query { for x in s do
                            where (fn()) }

let getTop rowCount =
    rowCount
    |> fun cnt s -> query { for x in s do
                            take cnt }
```

If your background is in C#, you can do similar types of things with Func<T, TResult>, but the syntax can quickly become less than ideal.

To take advantage of this generic repository you also have to make a few changes in the controller code. The great news is that these changes actually allow your code to be more testable as a byproduct. Before I show you how to implement these changes in the controller, I need to explain a few additional functional concepts.

Understanding Pipelining and Partial Function Application

Function composition is one of the key weapons available to the F# developer. To put it simply, function composition is the chaining together of small, single responsibility functions to form more complex, multidimensional processes and algorithms. This technique allows you to create applications that accomplish complex tasks, while keeping out bugs, reducing maintenance concerns, and increasing the ability to understand the code.

You've already seen several examples of function composition in this book as any time the pipe-forward operator is used, a form of this concept is being applied. The pipe-forward operator causes the function or method that is first in the chain to be evaluated with the result of that evaluation passed as an argument to the next function or method in the chain. The code that follows provides a simple example:

```
let function1 () =
    "Hello "
let function2 firstString =
    firstString + "Daniel "
let function3 combinedString =
    combinedString + "Mohl"

let result = function1() |> function2 |> function3
printfn "%s" result
```

This code defines three functions cleverly named function1, function2, and func tion3. Next, each function is called and the final output is assigned to result. Lastly, the result is printed to the screen. The interesting aspects here are that function1 is evaluated and the result of that function is then passed into function2 as an argument. Once function2 is evaluated, the result of that evaluation is passed in as the argument to function3. This ultimately produces a typical "Hello world!" result with "Hello Daniel Mohl" printed to the screen.

This may seem a little elementary if you have been doing much F# development, but it's important to have a solid understanding of this foundational functionality before moving on to more advanced concepts.

F# provides other composition-related operators that I have not mentioned here. More information on operators such as ||>, <||, <|, >>, and << is available here (*http://bit.ly/fssymbolsandoperators*). We will discuss a few of these here and there throughout this book.

The next concept related to function composition that you need to understand before moving on is that of *partial function application*. F# allows functions that can be partially applied—known as *curried functions*—to be created by simply separating the function arguments by a space. Here's an example:

```
let function1 firstString secondString thirdString =
    "Hello " + firstString + secondString + thirdString
```

This function allows you to pass some or all of the arguments. If only some of the arguments are provided, then a new function will be returned that expects the additional arguments that were not included in the first call.

For example, the `partiallyAppliedFunc` in the following code will result in a new function that expects a single string argument:

```
let partiallyAppliedFunc = function1 "Daniel" "Mohl"
```

You can now take advantage of these concepts to allow the `GuitarsController` to use a more functional approach.

Making the Controller More Functional

Using function composition and partially applied functions allows you to modify the `GuitarsController` to take advantage of the new `Repository` module. I'll show the modified controller in full and then break it down:

```
namespace FsWeb.Controllers

open System
open System.Web.Mvc
open FsWeb.Models
open FsWeb.Repositories
open Repository

[<HandleError>]
type GuitarsController(context:IDisposable, ?repository) =
    inherit Controller()

    let fromRepository =
        match repository with
        | Some v -> v
        | _ -> (context :?> FsMvcAppEntities).Guitars
                |> Repository.get
```

```
new() = new GuitarsController(new FsMvcAppEntities())

member this.Index () =
    getAll() |> fromRepository
    |> this.View

override x.Dispose disposing =
    context.Dispose()
    base.Dispose disposing
```

The first change simply opens the Repository module in much the same way a namespace would be opened. This step is really only needed to improve the readability of the code. The next change is that the main constructor now takes an object that implements IDisposable and an optional repository. The biggest difference here is that the repository is now a function rather than an object. Type inference helps out a lot in this scenario by identifying the appropriate signature of the function based on usage. This keeps everything nice and concise. The use of a function instead of an object allows for any function that matches the signature to be passed in as the repository. This greatly simplifies isolated unit testing, which can be a pain point when using Entity Framework.

The next change you will notice is the fromRepository definition. This piece of code checks the incoming repository parameter. If nothing was provided for that parameter (which is the case for normal execution), a little prep work is done to generate a function that will then be used to retrieve data in the various controller operations. This showcases a practical example of both function composition via the pipe-forward operator as well as partial application of a curried function. The pipe-forward aspect is associated with the passing of context.Guitars to the Repository.get function. This causes Repository.get to be partially applied with the first parameter (i.e., context.Guitars) with a new function being returned that expects the final parameter to be applied at a future time.

 You could have written Repository.get as simply get since we previously opened the Repository module; however, I think the current approach makes the code more readable.

The parameterless constructor comes next, which instantiates a new FsMvcApp Entities and passes it to the main constructor. A repository is not passed in this case. This works to our advantage, since the default repository-related functionality is desired when running the web application.

The final interesting change uses the fromRepository function that came in through the main constructor as well as the getAll function in the Repository module to retrieve the data. The results are then passed to the view in the same way you passed them in the previous examples. One other interesting benefit of using F# that is shown in this example is how the flexibility that the language provides can make your code more readable. `getAll |> fromRepository` reads very much like how I would write or say this in English. I could have just as easily switched this up by using `fromRepository (getAll())` or `fromRepository <| getAll()`, but that would not have been as readable. F# gives ample options that allow you to choose the best approach to accomplish the job at hand.

Simplification with Pattern Matching

You now have a controller and repository that read well, are easy to maintain, and follow a slightly more functional paradigm, but F# has many other features that can provide even more benefits. In this section I'll show you just a little bit of the power of pattern matching with F#.

Pattern matching is a feature that allows you to control program execution and/or transform data based on defined rules or patterns. F# supports a number of different pattern types. You can find a full list here (*http://bit.ly/StTkUu*).

To explain how pattern matching can help in your ASP.NET MVC projects, I will walk you through the creation of a new page. This page is used to create a new `Guitar` record. To accomplish this, you will need to add a new ASP.NET MVC view as well as a few new controller methods. The following example provides the markup associated with the new view that is in a new file named *Create.cshtml*:

```
@model FsWeb.Models.Guitar
<!DOCTYPE html>
<html>
<head>
    <title>Create a guitar</title>
    <meta name="viewport" content="width=device-width, initial-scale=1" />
    <link rel="stylesheet"
        href="http://code.jquery.com/mobile/1.0.1/jquery.mobile-1.0.1.min.css" />
    <script src="http://code.jquery.com/jquery-1.6.4.min.js">
    </script>
    <script src="http://code.jquery.com/mobile/1.0.1/jquery.mobile-1.0.1.min.js">
    </script>
</head>
<body>
    <div data-role="page" data-theme="a" id="guitarsCreatePage">
        <div data-role="header">
            <h1>Guitars</h1>
        </div>
        <div data-role="content">
            @using (Html.BeginForm("Create", "Guitars", FormMethod.Post))
            {
                <div data-role="fieldcontain">
                    @Html.LabelFor(model => model.Name)
                    @Html.EditorFor(model => model.Name)
                    <div>
```

```
                    @Html.ValidationMessageFor(m => m.Name)
                </div>
            </div>
            <div>
                <button type="submit" data-role="button">Create</button>
            </div>
        }
    </div>
  </div>
</body>
</html>
```

Place this new file in the *Views\Guitars* folder of the C# web application project. As with the previous ASP.NET view example, this view-related markup is for explanation purposes only and should not be taken as an example of something that is "production-ready."

You need to add two new methods to the `GuitarsController` class. This is where the pattern matching magic comes into play. The following shows the new methods. The emphasized code showcases the pattern match expression:

```
[<HttpGet>]
member this.Create () =
    this.View()
[<HttpPost>]
member this.Create (guitar : Guitar) : ActionResult =
    match base.ModelState.IsValid with
    | false ->
        upcast this.View guitar
    // … Code to persist the data will be added later
    | true -> upcast base.RedirectToAction("Index")
```

Let's concentrate on the second method. This method will handle a POST that includes the information needed to create a `guitar`. The interesting thing here is the pattern match expression that is determining flow based on the validity of the passed-in model class, which is `guitar` in this case. You can basically think of the pattern match expression for this example as a `switch` or `case` statement. (This simple match expression could have been written as an *if…then…else* expression. You can learn more about such expressions here (*http://msdn.microsoft.com/en-us/library/dd233231.aspx*).)

You may have noticed that the `HttpPost` version of `Create` requires a cast to `ActionResult`. You can make this read a bit better by providing a simple function to do the upcast, such as:

```
let asActionResult result = result :> ActionResult
```

The function can then be used as follows:

```
guitar |> this.View |> asActionResult
```

This is great, but what if you need to check multiple things, such as model validity as well as validation of something specific to a property on the model? As a contrived example, perhaps you need to check for model validity as well as verify that the word "broken" isn't in guitar.Name. The only way to accomplish this with a switch statement is to implement nested checks. This can quickly cause code to get out of hand and make maintenance a nightmare.

With F# pattern matching we can easily solve this with code such as the following:

```
let isNameValid = Utils.NullCheck(guitar.Name).IsSome &&
                  not (guitar.Name.Contains("broken"))
match base.ModelState.IsValid, isNameValid with
| false, false | true, false | false, true ->
    upcast this.View guitar
| _ -> upcast base.RedirectToAction("Index")
```

The important thing that I want to point out about this code is how the pattern match expression has become much more than just a switch statement. The first line now defines a tuple that contains the first value of base.ModelState.IsValid and the second value of isNameValid. We can now pattern match against that tuple.

 The Utils.NullCheck(guitar.Name).IsSome code in the preceding pattern match example determines whether the provided guitar object is null. Based on this, an F# Option type is returned that indicates Some if the guitar object is not null or None if the object is null. Here is the code for the Utils.NullCheck function that provides this functionality, and represents another pattern match example that has slightly different syntax from what has been seen so far:

```
let NullCheck = function
                | v when v <> null -> Some v
                | _ -> None
```

The first pattern in the preceding example is matching against the previously described tuple. It also is using OR logic, which makes the code more succinct. The match will succeed if the tuple equals (false, false), (true, false), or (false, true).

 The name validation check in this example is here to showcase a few of the capabilities of F# pattern matching. A real requirement such as this would be better served with a custom validation attribute that could be placed on the model and potentially checked client-side as well.

Pattern matching has a whole host of other great features, including the ability to bind input data to values for transformation, implement more complex guard logic, and match against F# record types.

The ability to pattern match against F# records is one reason to prefer records over classes when possible. Other reasons include immutability, conciseness, and improved features for creating new records that vary from the original.

Related Advanced Topics and Concepts

I've shown you several ways to start taking advantage of F# in your ASP.NET MVC applications. Your controllers and models should now be succinct, readable, and more functional in nature. Some of the benefits shown provide subtle improvements. Others can greatly improve the readability and reliability of your application. One thing that you may not realize just yet is how F# can improve the maintainability of your code. One example of this is related to the code transformation process I took you through for making the application more functional. Throughout the process I made a number of changes to types associated with various methods and functions. Thanks to type inference, I generally only had to change the type or signature in one location and the rest of the code automatically picked up the change. This can be a big win!

In the next section, I will walk you through a few more advanced concepts that are not directly related to ASP.NET MVC solutions, but are often used in conjunction with F# ASP.NET MVC solutions.

Improving Responsiveness with Async Workflows

It's been long known that asynchrony is one of the keys to achieving responsive websites. F# provides a feature, called *asynchronous workflows* (also known as *async workflows*), that makes it very easy to make asynchronous calls from the server. The basic syntax is as follows:

```
async {
    let client = new WebClient()

    return! client.AsyncDownloadString(Uri("http://www.yahoo.com"))
}
```

The astute observer will notice that the async syntax looks a bit like the query syntax. This is because async is a computation expression just like query. There is a ton of power in computation expressions.

The ! (pronounced "bang") operator in the preceding example is telling the computation expression that this line will be doing something to the underlying implementation by calling specific functions (Bind and Return, in this case). An example of how to build a custom computation expression is provided later in this chapter.

This simple async example creates a new WebClient inside an async block. It then downloads the content from the provided URI without blocking the current thread. It should be noted that the async block returns a task generator that will not actually be executed until explicitly told to do so. You can execute the previous code with something like Async.Start.

 Tomas Petricek has an excellent series of blog posts (*http://tomasp.net/ blog/async-csharp-differences.aspx*) where he talks about the differences between async in F# and C# 5.0. It's a great read!

How could you use this in ASP.NET MVC? Well, for starters you could make any external calls from within controllers use this feature. A more common usage is to create an asynchronous controller. Tomas Petricek and Jon Skeet provide an example of this (*http://msdn.microsoft.com/en-us/library/hh304367.aspx*). Yet another example is to use async workflows in combination with MailboxProcessors to allow lightweight processes that can be used for a whole host of different tasks. The next section provides an example of this.

Caching with MailboxProcessor

The MailboxProcessor feature in F# is one of those things that feels like pure magic. The more you play with it, the more uses you will find for it. MailboxProcessor—which is commonly aliased as agent—combined with asynchronous workflows, provide the ability to spin up tens of thousands of isolated processes that can be strategically positioned to do your bidding. This means you can divvy out work to various Mail boxProcessors, similar to how you might use threads, without having to incur the overhead associated with spinning up a new thread. Additionally, MailboxProcessors primarily (though not exclusively) communicate through message passing, which allows you to eliminate the problems associated with multiple threads using shared state.

To accomplish its intended task, each MailboxProcessor has a virtual "message queue" that is monitored for incoming messages. When a message arrives, it can be retrieved from the message queue and processed however you choose. Generally, pattern matching is used to determine the type of message that has arrived so that it can be processed appropriately. Once the message has been processed, an optional reply can be sent to the sender of the message (either synchronously or asynchronously).

The following example uses a MailboxProcessor to hold cached data:

```
namespace FsWeb.Repositories

module CacheAgent =
    // Discriminated Union of possible incoming messages
    type private Message =
```

```
        | Get of string * AsyncReplyChannel<obj option>
        | Set of string * obj

    // Core agent
    let private agent = MailboxProcessor.Start(fun inbox ->
        let rec loop(cacheMap:Map<string, obj>) =
            async {
                let! message = inbox.Receive()
                match message with
                | Get(key, replyChannel) ->
                    Map.tryFind key cacheMap |> replyChannel.Reply
                | Set(key, data) ->
                    do! loop( (key, data) |> cacheMap.Add)
                do! loop cacheMap
            }
        loop Map.empty)

    // Public function that retrieves the data from cache as an Option
    let get<'a> key =
        agent.PostAndReply(fun reply -> Message.Get(key, reply))
        |> function
            | Some v -> v :?> 'a |> Some
            | None -> None

    // Public function that sets the cached data
    let get key value =
        Message.Set(key, value) |> agent.Post
```

This may seem a little intimidating at first, but with a little explanation it will all be clear.

Messages as a discriminated union type

The first type that is defined in the CacheAgent module, which is named Message, defines all of the messages that are valid to send to the cache agent. This type is using a feature of F# called *discriminated unions*, which provides the ability to specify related groups of types and values. In this specific scenario, the feature is especially well suited as it allows you to define the message contracts that can be handled by the agent. Discriminated unions also allow each defined type to contain a different signature, which provides a ton of additional power. Discriminated unions have many use cases, and I will show more examples of them throughout the book.

In the previous example, only the input message is being defined in the Message discriminated union type. If necessary, you could easily define reply message types with varying signatures, as shown in the following example:

```
    type private MessageExample2 =
        | Get of string * AsyncReplyChannel<Reply>
        | Set of string * obj
    and Reply =
        | Failure of string
        | Data of obj
```

The core agent

The core agent is defined directly after the `Message` type. It creates and immediately starts a new `MailboxProcessor` that constantly watches for incoming messages. An anonymous function is then defined that contains a recursive function named `loop`. This `loop` function takes a single parameter named `cacheMap`, which will be repeatedly passed to the function to provide the needed state management. The use of the async workflow provides the ability for the agent to continuously loop without blocking any of the other application functionality. It is within this asynchronous workflow that the agent's message queue is checked for new messages.

If a new message is found, pattern matching is used to determine the message type so that appropriate processing can be done. In the case of a `get` message type, the `cacheMap` is searched for an entry that contains the specified key. If the key is found in `cacheMap`, then the associated value is returned as `Some(value)`, else `None` is returned. Finally, the result is returned to the sender of the message.

Once again we see an `Option` type in use. Using an `Option` type for values that would otherwise be `null` makes your application more robust since it helps prevent `null` reference exceptions. You'll see a consistent theme within F# related to explicitly over implicitly. The `Option` type allows explicit definition of something having an assignment or not having an assignment, whereas `null` can mean either the value doesn't have an assignment or it's just in a default state.

If the message is of type `set`, then the provided key/value pair is added to `cacheMap` and the new `cacheMap` is passed as the parameter in the recursive call to the `loop` function.

Lastly, the recursive loop is kicked off with an empty `Map`.

The `cacheMap` value in the `MailboxProcessor` example is using the F# type named `Map`, which is an immutable data structure that provides basic dictionary types of features.

The rest of the code is primarily defining the public API that allows interaction with the agent. It's basically just a facade on top of the agent's API that arguably makes it a little easier to work with.

More information and a few more `MailboxProcessor` examples are available here (*http://bit.ly/control-mailbox*).

Using the new CacheAgent

Taking advantage of this new `CacheAgent` is quick and easy. Simply call the public `get` or `set` functions. You could easily add this directly to the desired action of any of the controllers, but it would be better to write this once in the `Repository` and provide flexibility to determine whether the cache should be used. The following updates to the `Repository` module do the trick, with the emphasized code showcasing what is new:

```
module Repository =
    let withCacheKeyOf key = Some key

    let doNotUseCache = None

    let get (source:IQueryable<_>) queryFn cacheKey =
        let cacheResult =
            match cacheKey with
            | Some key -> CacheAgent.get<'a list> key
            | None -> None

        match cacheResult, cacheKey with
        | Some result, _ -> result
        | None, Some cacheKey ->
                let result = queryFn source |> Seq.toList
                CacheAgent.set cacheKey result
                result
        | _, _ -> queryFn source |> Seq.toList

    let getAll () =
        fun s -> query { for x in s do
                            select x }

    let find filterPredFn =
        filterPredFn
        |> fun fn s -> query { for x in s do
                                 where (fn()) }

    let getTop rowCount =
        rowCount
        |> fun cnt s -> query { for x in s do
                                  take cnt }
```

The first two functions provide a readable way to indicate whether cache should be used. If it is to be used, then the specific cache key string is included. Here are some examples of the use of these functions:

```
let top2Guitars = getTop 2 |> fromRepository <| doNotUseCache

getAll() |> fromRepository <| withCacheKeyOf("AllGuitars") |> this.View
```

The use of the *backward pipe* (i.e., < |) operator in the preceding example causes the result of the value to the right to be passed as input to the function on the left.<?xml version='1.0'?> <indexterm><primary><| (pipe-backward) operator</primary></indexterm>

The code changes in the `get` function allow results to be retrieved from cache (if desired and available), retrieved from the database with the cache being set to speed up future requests, or always pulled from the database. The first pattern match checks to see if caching is desired. If `Some key` was provided, an attempt to retrieve the cache from the `CacheAgent` is conducted. The result of that attempt is bound to `cacheResult`. If no caching functionality is desired, then `None` is bound.

The next pattern match expression is checking for three scenarios:

- Some value came back from the cache, in which case that value is returned to the caller.
- No cache was found in the `CacheAgent`, but the caching functionality is enabled. This causes the query to be run against the database, the result to be stored in the `CacheAgent`, and the result to be returned to the caller.
- Caching is not desired for this call. This causes all requests to go to the database and nothing to be retrieved from or set in cache.

A full book could be written on the uses for the `MailboxProcessor`. This `CacheAgent` example alone could easily be extended to include features such as auto-cache expiration, failover, auto-refresh of cached data, distributed processing, eventing when data changes, cache removal, and so on. Examples of use cases outside of this `CacheAgent` include, but are certainly not limited to, any background processing for which you might normally use a background thread, daemons, CQRS type architectures, notification engines, and web socket server implementations.

Jumping on the Message Bus

You already built a `MailboxProcessor`, so you have a head start when it comes to writing F# code in your ASP.NET MVC application that sends and receives messages. In this section, I will expand on this concept by talking about how to use F# in combination with a message bus. A message bus provides a number of advantages, ranging from scalability to a naturally decoupled system to multiplatform interoperability. Message-based architectures that utilize a message bus focus on common message contracts and message passing. Does this sound familiar? It should, since `MailboxProcessor`s basically do the same thing, but at a smaller, more focused level. While there certainly isn't enough space in this chapter to cover this topic in exhaustive detail, the examples provided in the following sections will get you started.

To keep things simple, I've created a small library called SimpleBus that will be referenced throughout the rest of this chapter. It should be noted that while SimpleBus works well for the basic examples in this book, it is missing several key features, such as full publish/subscribe capability, transactional queues, request–response capability, correlated messages, multiple message types per queue, and much more. For production applications, I recommend using one of the numerous message/service bus options available via a quick and easy Internet search. While SimpleBus would need a few enhancements to be production-ready, the F# code used to interact with the bus and the concepts described could certainly be used as is to build a robust production application.

SimpleBus

The primary goal of SimpleBus is to allow the publishing of messages to a specified MSMQ endpoint, which can then be watched and consumed by another process. This lays the groundwork for a highly scalable, decoupled, message-based system. To handle the publishing of messages, I've defined a function named publish that takes a queue Name and a type that will be serialized (using a BinaryMessageFormatter) and sent to the queue:

```
let publish queueName message =
    use queue = new MessageQueue(parseQueueName queueName)
    new Message(message, new BinaryMessageFormatter())
    |> queue.Send
```

The function first creates a new MessageQueue, taking care to ensure that the memory associated with the MessageQueue instance will be marked for release after use. The desired queue name is provided as an argument to a parseQueueName helper function, which will be described later in this section. The output of the parseQueueName function is then provided as a constructor argument to MessageQueue. A Message type—which is in the System.Messaging namespace—is then instantiated with the body of that Message type set to the generic message object that was passed in as an argument. The Message constructor is also provided a new BinaryMessageFormatter instance, which will cause the message to be serialized to binary form. If this formatter were not provided, the default would be XmlMessageFormatter. BinaryMessageFormatter is used here to provide better performance and to allow the sending of F# record types. The new Message is then piped to the Send method of the MessageQueue instance.

Two helper functions assist during a call to publish:

```
let private createQueueIfMissing (queueName:string) =
    if not (MessageQueue.Exists queueName) then
        MessageQueue.Create queueName |> ignore

let private parseQueueName (queueName:string) =
    let fullName = match queueName.Contains("@") with
                   | true when queueName.Split('@').[1] <> "localhost" ->
                       queueName.Split('@').[1] + "\\private$\\" +
```

```
                    queueName.Split('@').[0]
           | _ -> ".\\private$\\" + queueName
    createQueueIfMissing fullName
    fullName
```

The `createQueueIfMissing` function checks for the queue, and if it doesn't exist, it then creates a nontransactional queue. MSMQ allows messages to be published to local queues as well as to queues on remote machines. This is determined by the provided queue name. The `parseQueueName` function looks at the provided queue name, determines whether the queue is local or remote, and formats the queue name appropriately. It then calls the `createQueueIfMissing` function to verify that the queue actually does exist and creates the queue if needed.

With the `publish` function and associated helpers defined, you have all that is needed to start pumping messages into a queue. Before I show an example of this, I'll quickly show and describe the `subscribe` function:

```
let subscribe<'a> queueName callback =
    let queue = new MessageQueue(parseQueueName queueName)

    queue.ReceiveCompleted.Add(
        fun (args) ->
            args.Message.Formatter <- new BinaryMessageFormatter()
            args.Message.Body :?> 'a |> callback
            queue.BeginReceive() |> ignore)

    queue.BeginReceive() |> ignore
    queue
```

The `subscribe` function provides a way to consume messages from a queue. It allows the distinction of a type that will be used to determine what type the deserialized message should be cast to. Like the `publish` function, it also takes a `queueName` as the first argument. Additionally, it takes a callback function that will be called whenever a new message is found in the queue.

The first thing `subscribe` does is create a new `MessageQueue` in much the same way as what was done for `publish`. The only real difference is that `queue` is bound with the `let` keyword rather than the `use` keyword. This is important because it means the function will not clean up after itself, causing you to have to explicitly call `Dispose()` on the returned queue when `subscribe` is used. This additional cleanup step is required since the `ReceiveCompleted` event potentially needs to have access to the queue long after the initial call to `subscribe`.

The `subscribe` function then creates an event handler that will be raised by `System.Messaging.MessageQueue.BeginReceive` whenever a message comes into the queue that is being watched. This event handler sets the message formatter. It then casts the body of the message to the designated type and passes it as an argument to the callback function. The `BeginReceive()` method is then called to allow the queue to continue to be monitored. You don't really care about the `IAsyncResult` value that is returned from `BeginReceive()`, so it is ignored.

 As I mentioned at the beginning of this section, this `SimpleBus` is not production-ready. For example, it would not currently handle multiple subscriptions in the same assembly. I intentionally left this out to reduce complexity. A simple example of a message bus F# implementation that is used in a production application is available here (*https://github.com/dmohl/FsBus*).

Publishing messages

Separation of concerns is important in all aspects of software development, and solutions built on message-based architectures are no exception. One common approach for achieving this is to follow a principle called *Command Query Responsibility Segregation* (CQRS). A key tenet of CQRS is to clearly separate commands (operations that cause state change) from queries (requests that simply provide data for read-only activities). This approach fits very nicely into concepts associated with a functional-first language like F#.

 Just to be clear, use of a message-based architecture is not strictly related to CQRS or vice versa. However, these do often coexist, and a number of the concepts associated with CQRS and/or other architectures that use message buses are excellent companions to many of the core tenets of F#.

To test out the `publish` functionality, you can follow the concepts of CQRS by creating a type that will be used as a command to create a new `guitar` record. Since message types will need to be available to both the publisher and the subscriber, it's best to place them in a separate assembly. In this example, I've named the new assembly `Messages`. The `CreateGuitarCommand` record that will be published is as follows:

```
namespace Messages

type CreateGuitarCommand = { Name : string }
```

You can now easily publish this message with `SimpleBus.publish`. To see this in action, you can finish up the `Create` method in the `GuitarsController`. The modified method is shown in the following code, with the new code emphasized:

```
[<HttpPost>]
member this.Create (guitar : Guitar) =
```

```
match base.ModelState.IsValid  with
| false -> guitar |> this.View |> asActionResult
| true ->
    {Messages.CreateGuitarCommand.Name = guitar.Name}
    |> SimpleBus.publish "sample_queue"
    base.RedirectToAction("Index") |> asActionResult
```

 You will need to make sure MSMQ is installed on the machine. Additionally, you will need to run Visual Studio in admin mode (at least once) in order to have the application create the needed queue.

This new code simply creates a new `CreateGuitarCommand` record, with `Name` set to the provided `guitar.Name`, and pipes it to `SimpleBus.publish`. In this particular case, the record expression could be shortened to `{Name = guitar.Name}` as type inference would have taken care of the rest. However, it's common for multiple commands to exist with the same value names, so it's best to qualify them. For example, a `DeleteGuitar Command` might look like this:

```
type DeleteGuitarCommand = { Name : string }
```

Consuming messages

Consuming messages from the queue isn't much harder than publishing them. Often messages are consumed and processed via appropriate code that is deployed in Windows services; however, the messages could just as easily be consumed and processed by a web application. To keep things simple, you can consume the messages that were just published via a console application. The code looks like this:

```
open Messages
open System

printfn "Waiting for a message"

let queueToDispose =
    SimpleBus.subscribe<CreateGuitarCommand> "sample_queue"
        (fun cmd ->
            printfn "A message for a new guitar named %s was consumed" cmd.Name)

printfn "Press any key to quite\r\n"
Console.ReadLine() |> ignore
queueToDispose.Dispose()
```

This console application subscribes to the queue expecting messages that will deserialize to a `CreateGuitarCommand`. A function is passed as the second argument to the `subscribe` function, which will simply print some text to the console including the guitar name value from the message. The last line of the code disposes the `MessageQueue` object.

Continuation-Passing Style

Although the consumer of the messages works well if nothing goes wrong, what happens if an error occurs while the message from the queue is being processed inside the `subscribe` function? As it exists right now, the subscription process would simply stop working, throw away the message, and not tell anyone. This obviously is not what we want. At the very least, we need to allow the message retrieval to continue, and notify the message consumer of the problem.

One way to accomplish this goal is through something called *continuation-passing style* (CPS). At the risk of oversimplification, continuation-passing style is an approach that causes functions (specifically actions, thus inverting the control flow) to call other functions on completion rather than returning immediately to the caller. The simplest example of this is a callback function, similar to what is already being done in the `subscribe` function—this is actually an explicitly passed continuation.

Can we use this approach to handle the error message scenario? Absolutely; by simply passing in a failure callback function that is called from the `subscribe` function when an exception occurs, the message consumer can be notified and can handle the scenario appropriately. To accomplish this, the `subscribe` method is modified as follows (the changes are emphasized):

```
let subscribe<'a> queueName success failure =
    let queue = new MessageQueue(parseQueueName queueName)

    queue.ReceiveCompleted.Add(
        fun (args) ->
            try
                args.Message.Formatter <- new BinaryMessageFormatter()
                args.Message.Body :?> 'a |> success
            with
            | ex -> failure ex args.Message.Body
            queue.BeginReceive() |> ignore)

    queue.BeginReceive() |> ignore
    queue
```

The `subscribe` function is now accepting two functions as arguments. The first will be called on success and the second will be called on failure. The only change required to call the `subscribe` function is to pass in the function to execute on failure:

```
let queueToDispose =
    SimpleBus.subscribe<CreateGuitarCommand> "sample_queue"
        (fun cmd ->
            printfn "A message for a new guitar named %s was consumed" cmd.Name)
        (fun (ex:Exception) o ->
            printfn "An exception occurred with message %s" ex.Message)
```

I'll show several more examples of this concept in use in Chapter 2, including how to use `Async.StartWithContinuations` to handle success, failure, and cancellation of asynchronous workflows.

Creating a Custom Computation Expression

I've shown a few different computation expressions throughout this chapter that are provided out of the box in F#. These computation expressions give F# a lot of power, but it doesn't stop there. F# also gives you the ability to create your own custom computation expressions. Before getting into this, though, it's worth taking a second to boil down the definition of a computation expression to its simplest form.

It's easiest to think about a computation expression as a type wrapper that has a pipeline of operations that can be executed on a given set of F# code. The operations in the pipeline are applied at different points during execution of the wrapped code. Additionally, specific operations within that pipeline can be instructed to execute based on how the wrapped code is called. This allows for the creation of composable building blocks that can contain very complex pipelines, but that are trivial to use.

To show how to build a simple computation expression, I will walk you through the creation of one named `publish`. Yep, you guessed it; this custom computation expression will publish messages to the queue much like the direct call to the `publish` function of the `SimpleBus` that we discussed in the preceding section. Before showing you how to build a custom computation expression, I'll show you what the syntax will look like during usage:

```
publish {
    do! SendMessageWith("sample_queue",
            {Messages.CreateGuitarCommand.Name = guitar.Name})
}
```

While computation expressions can quickly become very complex, the one that allows the preceding syntax is quite simple. The code is as follows:

```
module PublishMonad

// Define the SendMessageWith Discriminated Union
type SendMessageWith<'a> = SendMessageWith of string * 'a

// Define the PublishBuilder builder type
type PublishBuilder() =
    member x.Bind(SendMessageWith(q, msg):SendMessageWith<_>, fn) =
        SimpleBus.publish q msg
    member x.Return(_) = true

// Create the builder-name
let publish = new PublishBuilder()
```

The first piece of this code that we should discuss is the `PublishBuilder` type. You can give this type whatever name you prefer; however, the general convention is to name it as shown in this example, where the *builder name* (i.e., publish) is changed to Pascal-case and appended with the word `Builder`. The *builder type* (i.e., `PublishBuilder`) can define various methods, which can change the way the builder works. The `Bind` method is called when the `let!` or `do!` (pronounced "let-bang" and "do-bang") symbols are used in the computation expression. The `Return` method is required and is called in most cases. Since it is not really being used by the logic in this code, a simple hardcoded `Boolean` value is returned.

The real work in the `PublishBuilder` is happening in the `Bind` method. This method takes two arguments. The first is a value and the second is a function. For this example, only the first argument needs to be considered. This argument contains a value of the `SendMessageWith` discriminated union type that specifies both the desired `queueName` and the message to send to that queue. The `Bind` method then uses those values to call the `SimpleBus.publish` function.

The `Create` action in the `GuitarsController` that is used during an HTTP `POST` can now be changed to this:

```
[<HttpPost>]
    member this.Create (guitar : Guitar) =
        match base.ModelState.IsValid  with
        | false -> guitar |> this.View |> asActionResult
        | true ->
            publish {
                do! SendMessageWith("sample_queue",
                    {Messages.CreateGuitarCommand.Name = guitar.Name})
            }
            base.RedirectToAction("Index") |> asActionResult
```

While this example is similar in concept to the `trace` computation expression provided on the MSDN documentation web page (*http://msdn.microsoft.com/en-us/library/dd233182.aspx*), the typical custom computation expression is implemented in order to accommodate more complex scenarios. Examples of common usages are available here (*https://github.com/fsharp/fsharpx/blob/master/src/FSharpx.Core/ComputationExpressions/Monad.fs*). More information on building custom computation expressions is available here (*http://msdn.microsoft.com/en-us/library/dd233182.aspx*).

Summary

This chapter covered a large number of topics in a fairly short amount of space. You went from finding and setting up your first ASP.NET MVC 4 application with C# and F# to building a custom computation expression that pushes messages onto a message bus. You also learned how to use a number of different F# features to build better web applications. Some of these include discriminated unions, the `Option` type, `Mailbox`

Processors, pattern matching, async workflows, the query computation expression, and more. You will see how to use many of these features in other scenarios throughout the rest of this book, so if you don't feel 100% comfortable with them just yet, there will be more examples to come.

In the next chapter, I will walk you through several approaches and options for building services with F#. Primary focal areas will include WCF (SOAP), ASP.NET Web API, and various web micro-frameworks. Unit testing in F# will also be covered. As the great Bob Seger song states, "Turn the page."

CHAPTER 2

Creating Web Services with F#

Inside every large program, there is a
small program trying to get out.

—C.A.R. Hoare

Throughout my career, the things that intrigued me the most, such as design patterns, principles, and architectural approaches, often caused me to focus primarily on the service layer. With the heart of the application, and sometimes even the entire enterprise, encapsulated in these services, this also seemed like the most important place to be. While my focus has expanded over the years, those things that I found intriguing still drive most of my thinking. Additionally, services are still one of my favorite things to create.

With the shift that is moving many of those patterns, principles, and practices that we know and love to the client side, the role of services is changing. While this change should cause you to embrace client-side architecture and development with as much ferocity as you have the service layer, it doesn't remove the need or importance of services acting as the workhorses of a solution. If anything, the shift provides better separation of concerns and improves the ability to create services that have a laser focus on the tasks that they are best suited to accomplish. By breaking a solution into small pieces that do specific things very well, the solution becomes more maintainable, extensible, testable, and easier to understand. Alex MacCaw, in *The Little Book on CoffeeScript* (O'Reilly), said it well: "The secret to building maintainable large applications is not to build large applications."

In this chapter I will walk you through the process of creating various types of web services that are primarily built with F#. Many of the features that F# provides are especially well suited to building services. This chapter will also dive into different frameworks that assist in constructing services to meet your specific needs. Lastly, I will show you a few F# features and open source libraries and frameworks that will improve the unit tests you create when building these services.

Installing the Existing WCF Project Template

Windows Communication Foundation (WCF) is an extremely versatile set of libraries that enables applications and solutions to communicate and interact via services. Services are often built to promote reuse, contain and isolate the domain(s) of a solution, handle complex processing, and integrate with other systems. Additionally, services generally need to handle massive concurrency and can often benefit from parallelism. If you're looking for the right tool to handle a job description such as this, then F# should be jumping to the forefront of your mind.

As with most of the examples in this book, the best way to use F# to build WCF web services is to create a C# project that handles everything related to the entry point of the service and one or more F# projects to contain all of the logic within the service. For an easy-to-use project template go to the Visual Studio Gallery (*http://visualstudiogal lery.msdn.microsoft.com*) website and search for "fsharp wcf". Figure 2-1 shows the result of that search. To install the template, type in a name for the project that should be created, click OK, and click Install. This creates a solution with three projects:

Contracts
 Contains the service, operation, and data contract(s) for the service(s)

Services
 Provides the service logic implementation

Web
 Wires everything up and provides the *.svc* file(s)

Exploring the Output Code

Since most of the interesting aspects of this code are in the Contracts and Services projects, I will only be digging into these. While this template splits out these two concerns into separate assemblies, this certainly isn't a requirement. This is, however, a common approach in large applications. Additionally, it opens up the ability to use ChannelFactory to create a channel to a service endpoint rather than having to use *Svcutil.exe* to generate code for a client proxy. I'll show an example of this later in this section.

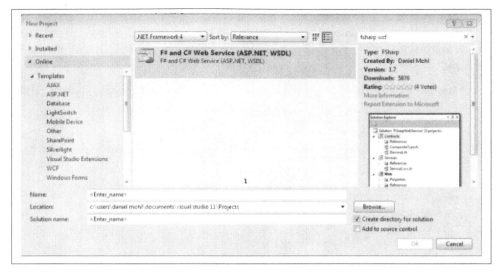

Figure 2-1. F# WCF template search on Visual Studio Gallery

The Contracts project provides two files. The first file contains a CompositeType, which gives an example of a record type that can be provided to and returned from a service operation. As I mentioned in Chapter 1, records should be preferred when possible; however, F# classes are also perfectly acceptable. The contents of this file are shown in the following example:

```
namespace FSharpWcfServiceApplicationTemplate.Contracts

open System.Runtime.Serialization
open System.ServiceModel

[<DataContract>]
type CompositeType =
    { [<DataMember>] mutable BoolValue : bool

      [<DataMember>] mutable StringValue : string }
```

 The template that I am currently walking you through is built to work for both F# 2.0 and F# 3.0. If you were targeting only F# 3.0, you could simplify the CompositeType record by using the CLIMutable attribute. I'll talk more about the CLIMutable attribute in Chapter 4.

As this example shows, the typical WCF attributes can be used with records in much the same way as how they are used in classes. Additionally, this example makes it clear that records do not have to be immutable, though they are by default. In this case, two mutable DataMembers are being defined: BoolValue and StringValue. While the lack of immutability in this case reduces some of the value of using a record type, you will still be able to retain some of the benefits. I'll talk more about the benefits of records a little later.

The other file in the Contracts project contains the ServiceContract and associated OperationContracts:

```
namespace FSharpWcfServiceApplicationTemplate.Contracts

open System.Runtime.Serialization
open System.ServiceModel

[<ServiceContract>]
type IService1 =
    [<OperationContract>]
    abstract GetData: value:int -> string
    [<OperationContract>]
    abstract GetDataUsingDataContract: composite:CompositeType -> CompositeType
```

This code defines an interface for the service. It's important to note that the emphasized code is not required in normal circumstances for defining an interface in F#, but it is required for WCF ServiceContract definitions. This is because WCF doesn't know how to handle parameters without an assigned name. Removing the emphasized code will allow the solution to compile, but will result in an error that states "All parameter names used in operations that make up a service contract must not be null. Parameter name: name" when the service is accessed. You can use any name you want for the parameters, but you must provide a name.

The implementation of the IService1 interface is provided in the Services project. As is the norm with F#, the code is very concise:

```
namespace FSharpWcfServiceApplicationTemplate

open System
open FSharpWcfServiceApplicationTemplate.Contracts

type Service1() =
    interface IService1 with
        member x.GetData value =
            sprintf "%A" value
        member x.GetDataUsingDataContract composite =
            match composite.BoolValue with
            | true -> composite.StringValue <-
                        sprintf "%A%A" composite.StringValue "Suffix"
            | _ -> "do nothing" |> ignore
            composite
```

After the Service1 type is defined, the interface that is being implemented is specified. Implementations for each operation specified in the interface are then added.

`GetData` simply takes the provided value, formats it, and returns the result. In this case, the formatting is taking the provided integer and returning the string representation of it. One thing to take away from this example is that F# provides a rich, extensible, type-safe family of functions that aid in formatting efforts. You can learn more about this here (*http://msdn.microsoft.com/en-us/library/ee370560.aspx*).

The `GetDataUsingDataContract` operation takes in a record named `composite`. It then sets `StringValue` on that object to a simple formatted string—if `BoolValue` is `true`—and returns the modified record to the caller. While it's generally a best practice to avoid mutation, the example shows how to accomplish it when required. A better approach would be to create a new record with the desired value that is then returned to the caller. I'll talk more about this later in this chapter.

Consuming the Service

You can easily consume this new service using a number of different approaches. If you are consuming the service from an F# application, the easiest approach is to use the `WsdlService` type provider, which is included out of the box in F# 3.0. To do this, simply add a reference to `FSharp.Data.TypeProviders` and add code such as the following:

```
open System.ServiceModel
open Microsoft.FSharp.Data.TypeProviders

type webService = WsdlService<"http://localhost:1555/Service1.svc?wsdl">

// This would be moved to a config file
let serviceUri = "http://localhost:1555/Service1.svc"

let client = new EndpointAddress(serviceUri)
             |> webService.GetBasicHttpBinding_IService1
printfn "The result was %s" <| client.GetData 100
```

 Depending on the project template used to create the preceding example, you may also need to add a reference to `System.ServiceModel`.

The use of the `WsdlService` type provider allows you to consume a web service without having to worry about running a separate code generator to create a client proxy. In this example, the `WsdlService` type provider is first provided a URI to the service's WSDL. This allows the type provider to generate the needed proxy types. An `EndPoint Address` is then created and passed into `GetBasicHttpBinding_IService1`. This lets you use one URI for development purposes, but override that URI via some external value, such as a config entry, when moving to other environments.

You may have noticed that for this example the WsdlService type provider also generates async operations by default. These aren't in the *Asynchronous Programming Model* (APM) style (i.e., Begin/End method pairs) that you may be used to, but they are operations that return a Task<'T> that can easily be awaited in an async workflow. This is known as the *Task-based Asynchronous Pattern* and, when combined with the asynchronous features of F#, it greatly simplifies asynchronous service calls. Here's an example:

```
open System.ServiceModel
open Microsoft.FSharp.Data.TypeProviders

type webService = WsdlService<"http://localhost:1555/Service1.svc?wsdl">

// This would be moved to a config file
let serviceUri = "http://localhost:1555/Service1.svc"

let client = new EndpointAddress(serviceUri)
            |> webService.GetBasicHttpBinding_IService1

seq {1 .. 20}
|> Seq.map (fun i ->
    async {
        let! result = Async.AwaitTask <| client.GetDataAsync i
        do printfn "The result was %s" result
    })
|> Async.Parallel
|> Async.Ignore
|> Async.RunSynchronously
```

The new code, which is emphasized, starts by creating a sequence of numbers that are then piped to Seq.map. The Seq.map function creates a new collection of asynchronous computations that will call the async version of the GetData operation and print the result when it returns. Since client.GetDataAsync returns a Task<'T>, we need to use Async.AwaitTask to convert it to an Async<'T>. The async computations are then set up to run in parallel, the result is ignored since we don't care about it, and the whole thing is launched. While the output from this console application will vary, the result should be something similar to what is shown in Figure 2-2.

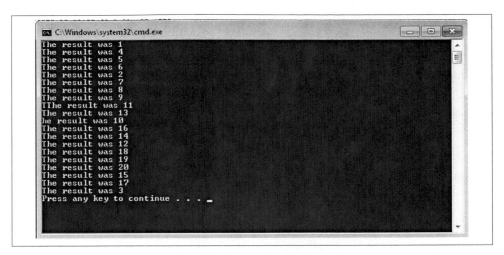

Figure 2-2. Parallel WCF calls with WsdlService type provider

In addition to the type provider approach, you have a few other options. One is to use *Svcutil.exe* to generate a client proxy that can then be referenced and used from the client. Another is to dynamically create a channel at runtime using ChannelFactory. To use the ChannelFactory approach, you'll need to first add references to the Contracts assembly as well as System.Runtime.Serialization. You then can use code such as the following:

```
open System.ServiceModel
open FSharpWcfServiceApplicationTemplate.Contracts

// This would be moved to a config file
let serviceUri = "http://localhost:1555/Service1.svc"

let address = new EndpointAddress(serviceUri)
let binding = new BasicHttpBinding()
let factory = new ChannelFactory<IService1>(binding, address)
let channel = factory.CreateChannel()
let clientChannel = channel :?> IClientChannel

try
    printfn "The result was %s" <| channel.GetData 100
    clientChannel.Close()
finally
    if clientChannel.State <> CommunicationState.Closed then
        clientChannel.Abort()
    clientChannel.Dispose()
```

This code programmatically creates a channel to the service after being provided an endpoint address and a binding. It then calls the GetData operation, prints the result, and closes the channel. Lastly, it checks the state of the channel, aborts it if it wasn't closed, and finally calls Dispose.

try/close/catch/abort WCF Client Pattern

Normally in F#, you could simply use the use keyword to dispose any object that implements IDisposable. However, there is a known issue when working with WCF, which causes the use of use to not work correctly. This is not something specific to F#, but rather something that is part of WCF. Because of this, a pattern known as try/close/catch/abort has been put into common practice. The F# code shown in the channel factory example effectively marks resources for disposal; however, it doesn't adequately handle exceptions. To fully implement the pattern, you could do something like the following:

```
try
    try
        printfn "The result was %s" <| channel.GetData 100
        clientChannel.Close()
    with
    | :? FaultException as fex -> printfn "Fault: %s" fex.Message
    | ex -> printfn "Error: %s" ex.Message
finally
    if clientChannel.State <> CommunicationState.Closed then
        clientChannel.Abort()
    clientChannel.Dispose()
```

Since the with part of the statement is a match expression, you can get even more creative and control specific error handling aspects outside of the exception type itself, as shown here:

```
try
    // This would be set in a config
    let enableLogging = true

    try
        printfn "The result was %s" <| channel.GetData 100
        clientChannel.Close()
    with
    | :? FaultException as fexl when enableLogging ->
        printfn "Fault Logging: %s" fexl.Message
    | :? FaultException as fex -> printfn "Fault: %s" fex.Message
    | ex -> printfn "Error: %s" ex.Message
finally
    if clientChannel.State <> CommunicationState.Closed then
        clientChannel.Abort()
    clientChannel.Dispose()
```

Because the try/close/catch/abort pattern is fairly verbose, it's common to move the logic into a separate method/function to support DRY. This is quite easy to do with F#'s support for functions as a first-class citizen. Here's an example:

```
let executeOperation action =
    try
        let enableLogging = true
```

```
            try
                action()
                clientChannel.Close()
            with
            | :? FaultException as fexl when enableLogging ->
                printfn "Fault: %s" fexl.Message
            | :? FaultException as fex ->
                printfn "Fault: %s" fex.Message
            | ex -> printfn "Error: %s" ex.Message
        finally
            if clientChannel.State <> CommunicationState.Closed then
                clientChannel.Abort()
            clientChannel.Dispose()

    executeOperation (fun () -> printfn "The result was %s"
                                  <| channel.GetData 100)
```

In this code, the `executeOperation` function takes a function named `action` as an argument that contains the desired code to execute. This allows the try/close/catch/abort pattern to be written once and reused whenever a service call is needed.

Diving into Records

I've mentioned records a few times in this chapter as well as in the preceding chapter. So far, the records we have seen in use for our WCF service have been mutable and I've repeated a few times that you lose certain benefits when using mutability. What are the benefits of records and what benefits are gained by immutability? How can we make some of the examples provided so far immutable rather than mutable?

F# records are data types that group a collection of named values. You can kind of think of them as a cross between a class and a struct. Records are reference types like classes, but they have structural equality like structs (which are value types). Like both structs and classes, you can optionally use instance and/or static methods with records. One big difference between records and classes/structs is that records are immutable by default. While we have to disable the immutability when using records with WCF, it's worth knowing what benefits we will lose by doing this. We'll start by looking at the benefits of immutability and then discuss the few benefits that are retained even when a record is forced to be mutable.

What does immutability buy you? Probably the biggest reason to lean toward immutability is that it makes your code easier to use in a concurrent and/or parallel manner. Writing this sort of F# application is pretty easy, but it can become disastrous if the underlying objects are shared and modified while being concurrently acted upon. You won't have to worry about this with immutable objects.

Immutability also allows provable testing that will always work exactly as expected. This makes your code easy to reason about and reduces difficult-to-track-down bugs that can be caused by data shifting around unexpectedly. Yet another advantage is that immutability gives the compiler free reign to rearrange the code during the compilation process to make it more efficient.

While immutable records are preferred, using them in our WCF service will result in an exception. Even though we've lost the benefits of immutability for this scenario, records still provide a few other benefits. These include pattern matching support as well as concise definition, creation, and copy syntax. Let's use these features to make our mutable record usage in the WCF service a little better. Here's the updated `GetData UsingDataContract` method:

```
member x.GetDataUsingDataContract composite =
    match composite with
    | { BoolValue = true; StringValue = _ } ->
        { composite with StringValue = "My New String" }
    | _ -> composite
```

This method now pattern matches against the record named `composite`. If `BoolValue` is `true` and `StringValue` is anything, then a new `CompositeType` record is created by copying the provided `composite` object and setting the `StringValue` to the value `My New String`. Since the pattern is really only checking that `BoolValue = true`, this can even be condensed a little more:

```
member x.GetDataUsingDataContract composite =
    match composite with
    | { BoolValue = true } ->
        { composite with StringValue = "My New String" }
    | _ -> composite
```

Building an ASP.NET Web API Service

ASP.NET MVC 4 includes a great new feature called ASP.NET Web API for building modern HTTP services. ASP.NET Web API is an evolution of the various REST APIs that the WCF team has developed over the past few years combined with many of the nice features provided by ASP.NET MVC. This convergence has resulted in an excellent platform for building HTTP services that supports a number of features such as content negotiation (i.e., XML, JSON, etc.), routes, conventions, testability, and more.

You may have noticed that the template used to create the ASP.NET MVC 4 web application in Chapter 1 includes an option for another template in the Project Creation Wizard. Building an HTTP service with ASP.NET Web API and F# is quite easy with the help of that same Visual Studio extension. Assuming you installed the Visual Studio

extension during the ASP.NET MVC discussion, all you have to do to create an F#/C#
ASP.NET Web API solution is to open the Project Creation Wizard and select Visual
F#→ASPNET→F# and C# Web Application (ASP.NET MVC 4). Then select WebApi
Project and click OK.

 At the time of this writing, the F#/C# ASP.NET Web API project template currently only supports the Razor view engine. The view engine
drop down will become disabled and will continue to show whatever
option was selected beforehand. Regardless of what this drop down indicates, the Razor view engine will be used.

Figure 2-3 shows the dialog just before you click OK.

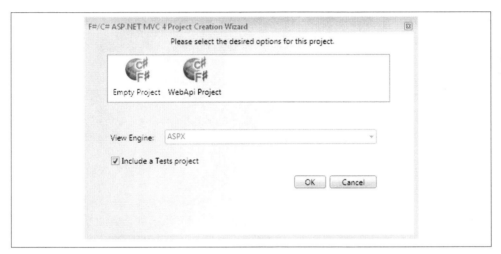

Figure 2-3. F#/C# ASP.NET Web API Project Creation Wizard

Analyzing the Template

The F#/C# ASP.NET Web API project template is divided into two primary parts:

ASP.NET MVC

The template includes a typical ASP.NET MVC application complete with a Home
view and a `HomeController`. The model isn't needed for the example application
provided by the template, so it has been left out. However, you can easily add it via
the usual approach if you need it. The ASP.NET MVC piece is optional. You could
completely remove it and still have the HTTP service(s).

ASP.NET Web API

> Alongside this typical ASP.NET MVC application is an HTTP service built with ASP.NET Web API.

I've already shown you quite a bit on using F# to build ASP.NET MVC applications, so I won't spend any additional time on this part of the template. The ASP.NET Web API portion of the template showcases an example of ASP.NET Web API in use. At first glance the code used to create the HTTP service could easily be mistaken for another controller provided for ASP.NET MVC. However, a slightly deeper inspection reveals several differences:

- There isn't a `View` that corresponds to the controller.
- There are differences in the *Global.fs* file.
- The controller inherits a different base class and the method names match the equivalent HTTP methods.

Like the other templates we've seen, F# provides the server-side code for this template. From a benefit perspective, the only thing F# is really providing in this simple, out-of-the-box state of the template is conciseness, but the nice thing is that you now have all the power of F# whenever you start implementing more complex functionality.

The changes to the *Global.fs* file are pretty simple. First a new record is created named `MapHttpRouteSettings` that will be used a bit later. The record declaration looks like this:

```
type MapHttpRouteSettings = { id : obj }
```

The `Global` class contains one new static method named `RegisterGlobalFilters`, which adds the `HandleErrorAttribute` to the global filters collection, as shown here:

```
static member RegisterGlobalFilters(filters:GlobalFilterCollection) =
    filters.Add(new HandleErrorAttribute())
```

We need to provide routing information for the HTTP services, so one additional method named `MapHttpRoute` is called in the `RegisterRoutes` method. There's no need to have an action placeholder in this route mapping, because by convention the ASP.NET Web API actions map to HTTP methods. This call looks like this:

```
routes.MapHttpRoute("DefaultApi", "api/{controller}/{id}",
    {id = RouteParameter.Optional}) |> ignore
```

Lastly, the `RegisterGlobalFilters` static method is added to the methods that are called in the `Start` method.

The main differences in the controller are that it inherits from `ApiController` instead of `Controller` and, as previously mentioned, the method names match up with the equivalent HTTP methods. Here's the `ValuesController` code:

```
namespace FsWeb.Controllers

open System.Web
open System.Web.Mvc
open System.Net.Http
open System.Web.Http

type ValuesController() =
    inherit ApiController()

    // GET /api/values
    member x.Get() = [| "value1"; "value2" |] |> Array.toSeq
    // GET /api/values/5
    member x.Get (id:int) = "value"
    // POST /api/values
    member x.Post ([<FromBody>] value:string) = ()
    // PUT /api/values/5
    member x.Put (id:int) ([<FromBody>] value:string) = ()
    // DELETE /api/values/5
    member x.Delete (id:int) = ()
```

Running the project will result in the display of the Home Index view. Navigating to a URL such as *http://localhost:[port]/api/values* provides a quick view of the result of calling the `Get` method.

If you prefer to self-host the services, you can do this quite easily as well. For example, to quickly create a console application that hosts the previously shown service, add references to `System.Net`, `System.Net.Http`, `System.Web.Http`, and `System.Web.Http.SelfHost`. You can now use code such as the following:

```
namespace WebApiServiceHost

open System
open System.Web.Http
open System.Web.Http.SelfHost

type ValuesController() =
    inherit ApiController()
    // GET /api/values
    member x.Get() = [| "value1"; "value2" |] |> Array.toSeq

module ServiceHost =
    type MapHttpRouteSettings = { id : obj }

    let main args =
        use config = new HttpSelfHostConfiguration(Uri "http://localhost:8080/")
        config.Routes.MapHttpRoute("DefaultApi", "api/{controller}/{id}",
            {id = RouteParameter.Optional}) |> ignore

        use server = new HttpSelfHostServer(config)
        server.OpenAsync().Wait()
```

```
        printfn "%s\r\n%s" "I'm ready to serve..."
            "Go to http://localhost:8080/api/values in a browser"
        Console.ReadLine() |> ignore

    main ()
```

 You must declare controllers in a namespace rather than a module.

The nice thing about using F# to create these services is that you now can use all of the great language features and examples that I have shown up to this point (and more) to build awesome HTTP services that return JSON or some other content type. Add the power of F# to standard scalability practices such as caching, distributed computing, and load balancing, and you have a winning combination that allows services that easily scale to massive proportions. Let's look at a few ways these services can be harnessed.

Interacting with the HTTP Service

One common approach for interacting with an HTTP service is to call it directly from the browser via JavaScript. Since this is slightly beyond the scope of this book, I won't spend a lot of time on the subject. However, just to show how easy it is, here's a little sample code:

```
<!DOCTYPE html>
<html lang="en">
<head>
    <meta charset="utf-8" />
    <title>ASP.NET Web API</title>
    <link href="@Url.Content("~/Content/Site.css")"
        rel="stylesheet" type="text/css" />
    <meta name="viewport" content="width=device-width" />
</head>
<body>
    <div id="sampleValues"/>

    <script src="@Url.Content("~/Scripts/jquery-1.6.2.min.js")"
        type="text/javascript"></script>
    <script src="@Url.Content("~/Scripts/modernizr-2.0.6-development-only.js")"
        type="text/javascript"></script>
    <script type="text/javascript">
        $(function() {
            $.getJSON( '/api/values' ).then(function( values ) {
                var sampleValues = [];

                $.each( values, function( i, value ) {
                    sampleValues.push( '<div>' + value + '</div>' );
                });
```

```
                    $( '#sampleValues' ).html( sampleValues.join('') );
                });
            });
        </script>
    </body>
</html>
```

This example was created by modifying the *Index.cshtml* file that's provided in the F#/C# ASP.NET Web API template.

This simple client-side code uses jQuery's `getJSON` function to call the `Get` method on the `ValuesController`. The results are then unceremoniously dumped on the screen. While obviously this example is lacking a lot of niceties, it does show how easy it is to interact with our new service directly from JavaScript.

What if you want or need to call the service on the server side? As is usually the case, F# gives you some great options for this! Let's start exploring…

Using HttpClient

While the ability to consume the service from JavaScript is important, there are times when you need to consume the service server side. Some easy ways to do this are with `System.Net.WebRequest`, `System.Net.WebClient`, or `System.Net.Http.HttpClient`. Each of these options has pros and cons, but I've found that `HttpClient` provides the most power with the least amount of required code. To get set up to consume our service with the `HttpClient`, create a new F# console application and install the `Microsoft .AspNet.WebApi.Client` NuGet package or add references to `System.Net.Http`, `System.Net.Http.Formatting`, and the `Json.NET` library.

`System.Json` is known to be pretty slow. Prior to the release candidate version of ASP.NET MVC 4, `System.Json` was the default. However, this was changed to `Json.NET` in the release candidate. Dave Ward talks about this more here (*http://encosia.com/jquery-asp-net-web-api-and-json-net-walk-into-a-bar/*).

You can now create a very simple implementation with code such as this:

```
open System
open System.Net.Http
open System.Json

let client = new HttpClient()
```

```
async {
    let! res = Async.AwaitTask
                <| client.GetAsync("http://localhost:5551/api/values")
    let! content = Async.AwaitTask <| res.Content.ReadAsStringAsync()
    printfn "The result is %s" content
} |> Async.Start

printfn "Please Wait..."
Console.ReadKey() |> ignore
```

This example uses the `GetAsync` method to call our service and await the result. It then asynchronously reads the content as a string. Running this example quickly shows the nonblocking, asynchronous nature of this call as "Please Wait…" is printed to the screen and the results of the service call are printed thereafter.

While the preceding example works well, consider what would happen if the overloaded `Get` method in the `ValuesController` looked like the following code, which returns a string if the provided `id` value is 1 or 2 and throws a 404 for anything else:

```
member x.Get (id:int) =
    match id with
    | 1 | 2 -> sprintf "Value is %i" id
    | _ -> raise <|
        HttpResponseException(new HttpResponseMessage(HttpStatusCode.NotFound))
```

After this change to the service, the consumer example that was just presented will sit in a waiting pattern if a URI such as *http://localhost:5551/api/values/3* is used. There are a few approaches we can take to resolve this. One is to add a call to the `EnsureSuccess StatusCode` method on the response. We can then simply add a try/with around the call, as shown here:

```
async {
    try
        let! res = Async.AwaitTask
                    <| client.GetAsync("http://localhost:5551/api/values/3")
        res.EnsureSuccessStatusCode() |> ignore
        let! content = Async.AwaitTask <| res.Content.ReadAsStringAsync()
        printfn "The result is %s" content
    with
    | ex -> printfn "%s" ex.Message
} |> Async.Start
```

Another approach is to use continuation-passing style to handle the error. Here's an example:

```
let task = async {
    let! res = Async.AwaitTask
                <| client.GetAsync("http://localhost:1232/api/values/3")
    res.EnsureSuccessStatusCode() |> ignore
    return! Async.AwaitTask <| res.Content.ReadAsStringAsync()
}
```

```
Async.StartWithContinuations(
    task,
    (fun r ->
        seq { yield "The returned values are:" }
        |> Seq.append <| JsonConvert.DeserializeObject<seq<string>>(r)
        |> Seq.reduce (fun acc v -> sprintf "%s %s" acc v)
        |> printfn "%s"),
    (fun err ->
        printfn "The request was NOT successful with error %s" err.Message),
    (fun canc -> printfn "The request was cancelled"))
```

`Async.StartWithContinuations` takes an asynchronous task as the first of the tupled arguments. The second, third, and fourth tupled arguments provide functions that indicate what should be done on completion of the async task, depending on the outcome of that task. If the task is successful, the first of the three functions is executed. If an error occurs, the second function executes. In the event of a cancellation, the third function is executed.

The code in the function that will be executed upon success is also worth discussing as it shows an example of using `Json.NET` to deserialize the response as well as an example of one approach for string concatenation without having to explicitly maintain state. The first piece of code creates a sequence with the initial value of the string we are creating. The response is then deserialized into a sequence of strings and appended to the initialization sequence, which causes a new sequence to be created that contains the combined values. Next we loop over the sequence of strings and reduce it down to a single string by adding each new value to the accumulator. Lastly, the accumulated result is printed to the screen.

The JSON type provider

While the `HttpClient` approach works pretty well, it can still be a bit of a pain to work with the JSON or XML that comes back from the service request. In order to work with these results in a type-safe way, you have to hydrate the result into an object or collection of objects. If you control both sides, this isn't a big deal since you've already created the model records or classes.

It becomes more difficult when you don't control the service implementation. Take, for example, a client that wishes to consume the iTunes API. Since the iTunes API returns JSON, you would have to manually create records or classes, call the iTunes HTTP service, and map the results of that call into those records or classes. It would be so much easier if there was a way to achieve the benefits of strong typing without having to manually build that entire boilerplate infrastructure.

As mentioned previously, F# 3.0 provides a feature, called type providers, that does just that. While the previously discussed type providers are provided out of the box, the one I'm about to show you was built by the community. It's available in an open source collection of libraries known as FSharpx (*https://github.com/fsharp/fsharpx*). The specific library that contains the JSON type providers is known as `FSharpx.TypeProviders` and it's available through NuGet via that same ID. You can read more about this type provider here (*http://www.navision-blog.de/2012/03/25/typed-access-to-json-and-xml/*).

Use of the JSON type provider to allow strongly typed access to the results from a simple iTunes search is pretty straightforward. You first navigate to the desired iTunes URI (*http://itunes.apple.com/search?term=guitar&limit=5*) and grab a sample of what the result of the service call will look like. You can either embed these results into the type definition or place them in a file, which is then referenced in that type definition. Once that's done it's as easy as calling the service and accessing the result. Here's an example that is using a version of `FSharpx.TypeProviders` that is later than 1.5.8:

```
open System
open System.Net.Http
open FSharpx

type itunesApi = StructuredJSON<FileName="itunesSample.json">

let client = new HttpClient()

async {
    let! res = Async.AwaitTask
                   <| client.GetAsync(
                          "http://itunes.apple.com/search?term=guitar&limit=5")
    let! content = Async.AwaitTask <| res.Content.ReadAsStringAsync()
    let root = itunesApi(documentContent = content).Root
    printfn "%i results were found." root.ResultCount

    root.GetResults()
    |> Seq.iter(fun x ->
            printfn "Artist Name is '%s' and Collection Name is '%s'"
                x.ArtistName x.CollectionName)
} |> Async.Start

printfn "Please Wait..."
Console.ReadKey() |> ignore
```

Before we leave ASP.NET Web API

In looking at the various clients we've built, you can probably see how the code could be considered to fit into the functional paradigm. One thing that may not be readily apparent is that most aspects of ASP.NET Web API, including the server-side aspects, are implemented in a functional manner. Ryan Riley has a nice post (*http://wizardsofs mart.net/post/the-functional-nature-of-web-api/*) that goes into this a bit. As he mentions, `HttpMessageHandlers` are at the root of everything when dealing with ASP.NET Web API. `HttpMessageHandlers` use the delegator pattern to allow for chaining of handlers. This pattern falls right in line with many of the concepts I already mentioned in this book.

We'll come back to ASP.NET Web API later in this chapter, when we discuss the topic of testing.

Exploring Other Web Frameworks

While ASP.NET Web API is a great framework for building HTTP services, for one reason or another it may not be for you. In this section I'll go over a few other popular options that allow the creation of HTTP services in F#.

Service Stack

Service Stack is an open source web services framework that can be found here (*https://github.com/ServiceStack/ServiceStack*) and here (*http://www.servicestack.net/*). It focuses on providing a framework for building high-performing web services created with a pattern-driven, code-first approach. The Service Stack umbrella also houses various optional projects that dovetail well with the core of Service Stack including, but not limited to, `ServiceStack.Text`, `ServiceStack.Redis`, and `ServiceStack.OrmLite`.

Standing up a minimal web service with F# and Service Stack is very easy. Simply install the `ServiceStack` NuGet package in a new F# application project and add a reference to `System.Web`. This allows you to create a self-hosted service with code such as this:

```
open System
open ServiceStack.ServiceHost
open ServiceStack.WebHost.Endpoints
open ServiceStack.ServiceInterface

[<RestService("/api/values/{Id}")>]
type ValueRequest = { mutable Id : int }

type ValueResponse = { Result : string }

type ValuesService() =
    inherit RestServiceBase<ValueRequest>()
    override x.OnGet request =
        { Result = sprintf "The value is %i" request.Id } |> box

type AppHost() =
    inherit AppHostHttpListenerBase("ValuesService",
                                    typeof<ValuesService>.Assembly)
    override this.Configure container = ()

module ServiceHost =
    let main args =
        use appHost = new AppHost()
        appHost.Init()
        appHost.Start "http://localhost:9090/"
```

```
    printfn "The service has started on port 9090"
    Console.ReadLine() |> ignore

main ()
```

The first important line of code is the definition of the `ValueRequest` *data transfer object* (DTO). For this example, the route is being established via an attribute on this DTO. As the name suggests, the `ValueRequest` object is provided as input during specific service calls. This F# record must have each named value marked as mutable to be used with the Service Stack infrastructure. If you prefer, you can use a class instead of a record for this. Additionally, the names of the values need to match the names of any associated replacement values specified in a route.

The `ValuesService` type provides the main implementation for the HTTP service. In this case, we've inherited from `RestServiceBase` to provide the service functionality, but we could have just as easily inherited `ServiceBase` or implemented `IService<T>`. The `OnGet` override provides the functionality that will be executed when a `GET` request is received. In this case, we are simply creating an instance of the `ValueResponse` record and returning it.

The `AppHost` type provides the code to set up and configure the service host. Lastly, the code in the `ServiceHost` module creates the service host, specifies the port to listen on, and kicks everything off.

If you're not a fan of decorating your request DTOs with attributes, you can establish routes in much the same way as you do for ASP.NET Web API. To do this, change the `AppHost` type to look like the following and remove the attribute from the `Value Request` type:

```
type AppHost() =
    inherit AppHostHttpListenerBase("ValuesService",
                                    typeof<ValuesService>.Assembly)
    override this.Configure container =
        base.Routes.Add<ValueRequest>("/api/values/{Id}") |> ignore
```

To consume the service, install the `ServiceStack` NuGet package and set up some code similar to the following:

```
open System
open ServiceStack.ServiceClient.Web

type ValueResponse = { mutable Result : string }

let client = new JsonServiceClient("http://localhost:9090")
client.GetAsync<ValueResponse>("/api/values/1",
    (fun r -> printfn "Result is %s" r.Result),
    (fun r ex -> raise ex) )

printfn "Please Wait..."
Console.Read() |> ignore
```

There's not much to it. In this case, we're instantiating a client of type JsonService Client, but there are a number of other options to choose from, including XmlService Client, WcfServiceClient, and Soap12ServiceClient. A full list with full source can be found in the GitHub codebase (*https://github.com/ServiceStack/ServiceStack/tree/ master/src/ServiceStack.Common/ServiceClient.Web*).

Once the client is created we have a few options for calling the service, depending on the type of client that is used. In this case, we're using an async version of methods with names that match up with the standard HTTP methods. Once again we see continuation-passing style in use. The first argument establishes the route to call. The second creates a function that will be executed upon successful completion of the call. This function includes an argument that represents the response, which will be of type ValueResponse in this example. The last argument provides a function that will be executed in the event of an error. It includes the response as well as an exception as input arguments. In the case of this example, we are simply rethrowing the exception that is provided.

 When you own both the client and the server implementations, it's common to provide the types in a separate assembly that is shared between both projects, rather than duplicating the type as I have done for ValueResponse. While this server implementation doesn't require ValueResponse to be mutable, the client implementation does. Because of this, the mutable version would be required in a shared assembly.

Nancy

Nancy is an open source framework for building HTTP services in .NET. It was built from the ground up to provide a simple and lightweight mechanism for standing up services that can be hosted almost anywhere. Additionally, it supports a number of out-of-the-box view engine integrations that allow you to easily utilize Nancy for your standalone HTTP service needs as well as for a full web framework (if desired).

To stand up a simple service host, create a new F# console application, install the Nancy.Hosting.Self NuGet package, and add code such as the following:

```fsharp
open System
open Nancy
open Nancy.Hosting.Self

let GetNancyParam prms key = (prms :> DynamicDictionary).[key]

type System.String with
    static member toNancyResponse (s:string) = Response.op_Implicit s

type ValuesModule() =
```

```
    inherit NancyModule()
    let getResponse v = v |> sprintf "The response is %A"
                          |> String.toNancyResponse
    do base.Get["/api/values"] <-
        fun _ -> ["value1", "value2"] |> getResponse
    do base.Get["/api/values/{id}"] <-
        fun prms -> (unbox prms, "id") ||> GetNancyParam |> getResponse

let host = NancyHost( Uri "http://localhost:9191" )
host.Start()

printfn "The service is running on port 9191..."
Console.ReadKey() |> ignore

host.Stop()
```

From a lines-of-code perspective, this is one of the shortest implementations that we've seen so far. However, it is also the most complex. That being said, it's still fairly readable once you get a full picture of what is going on. Let's break it down…

The first function, named `GetNancyParam`, is a helper function used to get a parameter value out of the `DynamicDictionary` type that Nancy uses to store any values coming in from the request that are specified as replaceable parameters in the routes. As with other aspects of the language (such as mutability), F# doesn't like for things to automatically change under the covers. Instead, it takes the approach of requiring explicit instruction from the developer for an action that causes a change that might otherwise not be expected. The requirement to cast to a type or interface rather than automatically converting to that type or interface is an example of this. The `GetNancyParam` function explicitly casts the provided `prms` (short for parameters) argument to a `Dynamic Dictionary`. It then retrieves the value based on the provided key (which is `id` in this case).

The next few lines show a feature of F# that I haven't yet talked about, called *type extensions*. Type extensions give you the ability to add new functionality to an existing type. The type extension in this example extends `System.String` to allow conversion of the given string to a Nancy `Response` object. This conversion is required since Nancy only allows a `Response` object or one of several implicit cast operators to be returned. You can find more information here (*https://github.com/NancyFx/Nancy/wiki/Defining %20routes*).

Now we set up our Nancy module class. Nancy modules are the primary means by which services are created. As the example shows, all we need to do to create a Nancy module is to define a class that inherits from `NancyModule`. We next define a function within the class that helps convert a provided value into whatever string we want to output. This shows a nice feature of F#. This function is now scoped to only this class. This is also known as a *closure*. Closures are often used to encapsulate functionality and/or state. Additionally, they can be very useful in creating DRY code.

Now a few routes are established. Since routes are set up in the constructor of classes when using Nancy, we need to use the *do binding* to implement this in F#. Do bindings can be static or nonstatic and they execute in the order in which they are placed in the class. The first defined route simply returns a string representation of a list of strings.

It is possible in F# to set up a constructor with an optional then keyword to initialize various aspects of the object. However, the do binding is the preferred approach.

The second defined route returns a string that includes the `id` value that was provided in the request. It has a couple of interesting aspects. First, it uses the `unbox` function to cast the reference type instance back to the original value type. This can then be passed to the `GetNancyParam` function and cast to a `DynamicDictionary`. The second interesting thing is the use of the *double forward pipe* operator, `||>`. This operator takes a tuple of two values on the left that is then deconstructed and passed in as two arguments to the function on the right. This line could have also been written as:

```
fun prms -> GetNancyParam (unbox prms) "id" |> getResponse
```

Both Nancy and Service Stack work well with F# and you can certainly use F# to build solid HTTP services with these two frameworks. In fact, the concise yet readable nature of F# makes it a great option even if that's the only reason you choose to use it. That being said, these two frameworks are certainly targeted at the object-oriented paradigm, and as such, you can't take full advantage of all the features of F#. There are a few options if you wish to create web stacks with more idiomatic F# code. A few of these include Figment (*https://github.com/mausch/Figment*) by Mauricio Scheffer, PicoMvc (*https://github.com/robertpi/PicoMvc*) by Robert Pickering, and Frank (*https://github.com/frank-fs/frank*) by Ryan Riley. In the interest of space, I will only provide an example of one of these.

It's important to point out that you don't have to currently be a functional programming ninja to use F#. As I mentioned in the preceding paragraph, you may choose to use F# only for the benefits of type inference and terseness. There's no wrong way; simply pick and choose what works for you. You'll often find that once you start using F#, it will help move you to the "right" path. If you wish to learn more about how to make your code more functional, Richard Minerich has a great post (*http://bit.ly/functional-programming*) to get you started.

Frank

The original plan for Frank was to create a framework similar to Sinatra, but with a focus on functional principles and techniques. It was paired with another library called Frack that was intended to provide middleware functionality to complement web application frameworks such as Frank. However, Ryan Riley (the creator of Frank and Frack and a technical editor of this book) felt that ASP.NET Web API really got it right. Because of this, he changed Frank to simply be a functional wrapper around `System.Net.Http` that focuses primarily on function composition. Frack is no longer an active project, but many of its features have been ported into Frank.

Here's an example of a simple self-hosted Frank service:

```
open System
open System.Net
open System.Net.Http
open System.Web.Http
open System.Web.Http.SelfHost
open Frank

let values request =
    respond HttpStatusCode.OK
        <| new StringContent(["values1"; "values2"].ToString())
        <| ignore
    |> async.Return

let value request =
    let id = getParam request "id"
    respond HttpStatusCode.OK
        <| new StringContent(sprintf "The value is %s" id)
        <| ignore
    |> async.Return

let app = merge [ route "/api/values" <| get values
                  route "/api/values/{id}" <| get value ]

module HostServer =
    let main args =
        let baseUri = "http://localhost:9393"
        use config = new HttpSelfHostConfiguration(baseUri)
        config.Register app

        use server = new HttpSelfHostServer(config)
        server.OpenAsync().Wait()

        printfn "The service is running at %s..." baseUri
        Console.ReadKey() |> ignore
        server.CloseAsync().Wait()

    main ()
```

The most important lines of code for this implementation are emphasized. Let's go through this emphasized code function by function. The first function, named `values`, is defining what will be returned when the `/api/values` route is hit.

There are two main pieces to the `values` function. First, it defines the response that should be sent back for the specific request. This response is being composed with the help of the backward pipe operator for composition and the `response` function from Frank. The `response` function is being provided an HTTP status code of 200 (`OK`) and the string representation of the provided array of strings as content. The last thing that can be sent to the response function is a function that will add various headers to the response. Frank has a number of these functions built in; however, in this case we don't need them, so `ignore` is being provided.

The second main aspect of the `values` function is the piping of the output of the response function to `async.Return`. This function is part of the `AsyncBuilder` type in F#. This whole thing could have also been wrapped in an async block to achieve the same effect, as shown in the following example:

```
let values request = async {
    return respond HttpStatusCode.OK
        <| new StringContent(["values1"; "values2"].ToString())
        <| ignore
}
```

The `value` function in the earlier code contains much of the same functionality as the `values` function in the preceding code. However, it has the added ability to react appropriately to placeholder parameters provided in the URI. The `getParam` function included in Frank provides the core functionality to accomplish this. Pass in the placeholder key that was specified in the route, `id` in this case, and the value that was provided in the URI will be returned. This example merely spits back the value that was provided in the URI, but the logic can easily become as complex as needed.

The last point of interest is the code that defines the routes. In this example, `app` is bound to the output of the `merge` function that is provided as part of Frank. The `merge` function takes a sequence of type `HttpResource`. An `HttpResource` is made up of route information, a definition of what HTTP methods are allowed for that route, and a designation of which function should be used to handle a given request. In this case, I'm only allowing the `GET` HTTP verb for these two routes. To add support for the `DELETE` HTTP verb (or one of the others that are supported), you only need to define a function to handle that request and update the information that is passed to the `merge` function. Here's an example with the new code emphasized:

```
let delValue request =
    new HttpResponseMessage() |> async.Return

let app = merge [ route "/api/values" <| get values
                  route "/api/values/{id}" <| (get value <|> delete delValue)]
```

One of the big benefits of Frank is the distinct advantage of function composition. This allows very easy addition of new functionality. As an example of this, I'll show you how to add logging to all of the request handlers. This example uses one of the out-of-the-box middleware functions provided in Frank:

```
let app = merge [ route "/api/values" <| get values
                  route "/api/values/{id}" <| get value]
         |> Middleware.log
```

The addition of the one new line shown in this example allows all requests to now have basic trace logging enabled, including tracking of how long the request takes. While Frank provides a few of these middleware functions out of the box, it's also very easy to create your own custom middleware. The main Frank GitHub page (*https://github.com/frank-fs/frank*) has information on how to do this.

Adding Binding Redirection

Since Frank is written with F# 2.0 as the target, one extra step is necessary when using it with F# 3.0. You must set up binding redirects from previous versions of FSharp.Core to FSharp.Core version 4.3.0.0. You can certainly do this by hand, but NuGet provides an even easier option. Add a config file to the project and then run the following command in the NuGet Package Manager Console (which you can find in Visual Studio under View→Other Windows→Package Manager Console) replacing *projectname* with the name of the desired project:

```
Add-BindingRedirect projectname
```

This will update the config file to include something like the following:

```xml
<?xml version="1.0" encoding="utf-8"?>
<configuration>
  <runtime>
    <assemblyBinding xmlns="urn:schemas-microsoft-com:asm.v1">
      <dependentAssembly>
        <assemblyIdentity name="FSharp.Core"
          publicKeyToken="b03f5f7f11d50a3a" culture="neutral" />
        <bindingRedirect oldVersion="0.0.0.0-4.3.0.0"
          newVersion="4.3.0.0" />
      </dependentAssembly>
    </assemblyBinding>
  </runtime>
</configuration>
```

You will need to do this for any F# 3.0 projects that utilize libraries built with earlier versions of F#, so keep this command close by.

You can get a complete solution that contains this example on my GitHub (*https://github.com/dmohl/fs-web-cloud-mobile*).

Testing Your Creation

In the first chapter, I briefly mentioned the importance of creating solutions that are easy to test. A few of the sections in that chapter provide various techniques that you can apply in F# to make your solutions more testable. However, I didn't go into any detail regarding approaches to create unit tests in F# and/or specific features of F# that can improve this process.

In this section, I'll walk you through the tools and techniques you can use to unit-test your F# masterpieces. I'll also showcase a few frameworks that can make this testing easier and/or more enjoyable.

Getting Set Up

For many of the examples in the next few sections, I'll be using an ASP.NET Web API controller and a repository that look pretty similar to some of the ASP.NET MVC examples you saw in Chapter 1. The controller looks like the following:

```
namespace FsWeb.Controllers

open System
open System.Web.Http
open Microsoft.FSharp.Data.TypeProviders
open FsWeb.Models
open Repository

type dbContext = SqlDataConnection<ConfigFile="Web.config",
                                   ConnectionStringName="FsMvcAppExample">

type DataContext = dbContext.ServiceTypes.SimpleDataContextTypes.FsMvcAppExample

type GuitarsController(context:IDisposable, ?repository) =
    inherit ApiController()

    let fromRepository =
        match repository with
        | Some v -> v
        | _ -> (context :?> DataContext).Guitars |> get

    new() = new GuitarsController(dbContext.GetDataContext())

    // GET /api/guitars
    member x.Get() =
        getAll() |> fromRepository |> List.toSeq

    override x.Dispose disposing =
        context.Dispose()
        base.Dispose disposing
```

The repository is a simplified version of what I showed previously:

```
module Repository

open System
open System.Linq

let get (source:IQueryable<_>) queryFn =
    queryFn source |> Seq.toList

let getAll () =
    fun s -> query { for x in s do
                        select x }
```

This controller and repository interact with the database that was also created in the first chapter. Since the database already exists, I've used the `SqlDataConnection` type provider to interact with it.

Another feature of F# that I haven't yet mentioned and that comes in handy here is *type abbreviations*. Type abbreviations, like the one named `DataContext` in the sample code, allow you to alias types in order to improve code readability. These help in a lot of scenarios, but can be especially useful when working with the types generated by type providers.

You can now quickly write a test that verifies that the `Get` method on the `Guitars Controller` will correctly return results from the database. If you included a test project when the ASP.NET Web API solution was created, you can now add references to your favorite testing framework. I'll use a few different ones throughout the following examples. This first example uses `MSTest`, and all you need to do to get set up is to add a reference to `Microsoft.VisualStudio.QualityTools.UnitTestFramework`.

 An F# `MSTest` project template is available on Visual Studio Gallery (*http://visualstudiogallery.msdn.microsoft.com/*) or via the Online Template Search functionality in Visual Studio 2012.

Now that the test project is ready to go, you can create a test with code such as the following:

```
module GuitarsControllerTests

open Microsoft.VisualStudio.TestTools.UnitTesting
open FsWeb.Controllers

[<TestClass>]
type Tests() =
    [<TestMethod>]
    member x.GetAllGuitarsTest() =
        use controller = new GuitarsController()
        let result = controller.Get()
        Assert.AreEqual(3, result |> Seq.length)
```

This code creates the controller, calls the `Get` method, and verifies that the number of returned values equals the expected value of 3.

You are probably waving your hand wildly right now with lots of ideas on how to improve this test. You're probably thinking that this test isn't all that readable, isn't isolated, will be slow due to the crossing of boundaries, and so on. If you are thinking anything along these lines, then you are absolutely right. This may be fine for an integration test, but it's lacking in the area of a quality unit test. In the next several subsections, I'll point out a few approaches, libraries, frameworks, and features of F# that you can use to improve this test.

Improving Tests with F#

How can we use F# to improve the test we just wrote? To start with, we can look at options for making the test more readable while also getting the code into a better place:

```
module ``Given a Guitars Controller``

open Microsoft.VisualStudio.TestTools.UnitTesting
open FsWeb.Controllers

[<TestClass>]
type ``When getting all the guitars from the repository``() =

    let controller = new GuitarsController()
    let result = controller.Get()

    [<TestMethod>]
    member x.``it should have a count of three``() =
        Assert.AreEqual(3, result |> Seq.length)
```

F# provides a great feature called a *double backtick* (` `` `) that allows a number of characters, that could not normally be used, to be included as part of an identifier. This allows you to go wild with creating very readable module, class, and method names. In the preceding example, this feature is used to allow the module, type, and method names to all include spaces. You'll see this feature used a lot in the upcoming examples with different libraries and frameworks.

Another feature of F# that will allow our example to no longer cross the boundary to the database and thus will make the tests more isolated is that of *object expressions*. Object expressions allow you to create an object with another object or interface providing a sort of template. You can then implement and/or override certain aspects of the new object or interface.

If this sounds a bit like the functionality you might expect out of a mocking library, then you are going down the right track. Here's an updated example (with new code emphasized) that makes use of an object expression to create a fake repository:

```
module ``Given a Guitars Controller``

open System
open System.Linq
open Microsoft.VisualStudio.TestTools.UnitTesting
open FsWeb.Controllers
open FsWeb.Models

type Guitar = dbContext.ServiceTypes.Guitars

[<TestClass>]
type ``When getting all the guitars from the repository``() =

    let fakeRepository =
        [| Guitar(Id = Guid.NewGuid(), Name = "test1")
           Guitar(Id = Guid.NewGuid(), Name = "test2")
           Guitar(Id = Guid.NewGuid(), Name = "test3") |]
        |> Queryable.AsQueryable
        |> Repository.get

    let context = { new Object()
                          interface IDisposable with
                             member x.Dispose() = () }

    let controller = new GuitarsController(context, fakeRepository)
    let result = controller.Get()

    [<TestMethod>]
    member x.``it should have a count of three``() =
        Assert.AreEqual(3, result |> Seq.length)
```

The first bit of code is creating a list of fake data to use for testing purposes. The list is then turned into something that we can query against and passed to the `Repository`
`.Get` function. When this is later passed into `GuitarsController`, it will be treated just as though it were data coming back from the database via the `SqlDataConnection` type provider.

The second interesting thing to notice is how the `IDisposable` aspect of `context` is being provided. Since we aren't using a repository that implements `IDisposable`, we have to fake it. We can easily do this with an object expression that creates an anonymous `Object` type and implements `IDisposable` with a `Dispose` member that doesn't do anything.

A number of frameworks have been built to take advantage of the syntax and features of F#. Throughout the next several sections, we'll briefly explore some of these frameworks.

FsUnit

FsUnit was originally created by Ray Vernagus back in 2007. Since that time, FsUnit has had various contributors. It's also gone on to include support for many of the most popular test frameworks including xUnit.NET, MbUnit, the originally supported NUnit, and most recently, `MSTest`.

The easiest way to get started with FsUnit is to install one of the available NuGet packages. For instance, to use FsUnit with MSTest, install the NuGet package with ID `Fs30Unit.MsTest`. This package pulls down the needed libraries, adds appropriate references, and provides a simple example of usage.

Once this is complete, you can rewrite the test method to use a much nicer and more readable syntax than the typical `Assert` approach. With FsUnit, our single test method becomes:

```
[<TestMethod>]
member x.``it should have a count of three``() =
    result |> Seq.length |> should equal 3
```

If we define a value that is bound to one of the items in the resultant sequence, we can create a test that checks for its existence, like this:

```
[<TestMethod>]
member x.``it should contain a specific guitar record``() =
    result |> should contain expectedGuitar
```

As I mentioned previously, FsUnit also supports NUnit, MbUnit, and xUnit.NET. One nice thing about working with one of these three frameworks is that you can create tests using more of a functional approach rather than an object-oriented approach. Here's an example of the same test written with FsUnit for xUnit.NET:

```
module ``When getting all guitars``

open System
open System.Linq
open FsWeb.Controllers
open FsWeb.Models
open FsUnit.Xunit
open Xunit

type Guitar = dbContext.ServiceTypes.Guitars

let expectedGuitar = Guitar(Id = Guid.NewGuid(), Name = "test1")

let fakeRepository =
    [| expectedGuitar
       Guitar(Id = Guid.NewGuid(), Name = "test2")
       Guitar(Id = Guid.NewGuid(), Name = "test3") |]
    |> Queryable.AsQueryable
    |> Repository.get
```

```
let context = { new Object()
                interface IDisposable with
                    member x.Dispose() = () }

let controller = new GuitarsController(context, fakeRepository)
let result = controller.Get()

[<Fact>]
let ``it should have a count of three``() =
    result |> Seq.length |> should equal 3

[<Fact>]
let ``it should contain a specific guitar record``() =
    result |> should contain expectedGuitar
```

Several keywords are available to allow you to craft your tests in the most readable way possible. You can find a full list as well as various examples here (*https://github.com/dmohl/fsunit*).

 As I mentioned previously in this chapter, libraries targeting F# 2.0 require a binding redirect to `FSharp.Core` 4.3.0.0. This is needed for FsUnit when using it with F# 3.0 and NUnit, MbUnit, or xUnit.NET. It's also needed for the Unquote and NaturalSpec examples, which I will talk about next.

Unquote

Unquote is another excellent library for creating unit tests in F#. It was written by Stephen Swensen; supports all exception-based testing frameworks such as xUnit.NET, NUnit, MbUnit, and MSTest; works within F# Interactive as well as with more traditional approaches; and primarily uses F#-quoted expressions to allow statically checked tests. It provides several useful operators to make your life as a developer a little easier. Additionally, clear and well-formatted error messages make this an excellent choice.

Getting started with Unquote is as easy as installing the `Unquote` NuGet package as well as the NuGet package of the desired testing framework. You can then create tests within a project or an FSI session. Here's an example of how to use Unquote and xUnit.NET to test our `GuitarsController`:

```
module ``Given a GuitarsController``

open System
open System.Linq
open FsWeb.Controllers
open FsWeb.Models
open Swensen.Unquote
open Xunit
```

```
type Guitar = dbContext.ServiceTypes.Guitars

let fakeRepository =
    [| Guitar(Id = Guid.NewGuid(), Name = "test1")
       Guitar(Id = Guid.NewGuid(), Name = "test2")
       Guitar(Id = Guid.NewGuid(), Name = "test3") |]
    |> Queryable.AsQueryable
    |> Repository.get

let context = { new Object()
                        interface IDisposable with
                            member x.Dispose() = () }

let controller = new GuitarsController(context, fakeRepository)

[<Fact>]
let ``When getting the guitars from the repo it should have a count of 3``() =
    test <@ controller.Get() |> Seq.length = 3 @>
```

The main difference here is the use of the `test` assertion operator, which is followed by a quoted expression. The quoted expression contains the code that should be decompiled, evaluated, and reduced. Reductions of expressions and subexpressions are conducted recursively until an exception is thrown or all are complete. Since Unquote primarily uses quoted expressions, you rely on all of the F# knowledge you currently have and really only have to learn three test assertion operators: `test`, `raise`, and `raiseWith`.

Downloads, documentation, examples, release notes, and other information on Unquote is available here (*http://code.google.com/p/unquote/*).

NaturalSpec

While there are several other excellent frameworks that help with testing in F#, I will only talk about one more in the interest of space. NaturalSpec is a *domain-specific language* (DSL) written by Steffen Forkmann that sits on top of NUnit. As the name suggests, NaturalSpec focuses on making it easy to create tests or specifications that flow in natural language, such as how you might describe the acceptance criteria in writing. It uses the pipe-forward operator heavily, and as such, makes for an elegant use of functions.

The example that follows once again tests our `GuitarsController`. The new code written to work with NaturalSpec is emphasized:

```
module GuitarsControllerTests

open System
open System.Linq
open FsWeb.Controllers
open FsWeb.Models
open NaturalSpec
```

```
type Guitar = dbContext.ServiceTypes.Guitars

let expectedGuitar = Guitar(Id = Guid.NewGuid(), Name = "test1")

let fakeRepository =
    [| expectedGuitar
       Guitar(Id = Guid.NewGuid(), Name = "test2")
       Guitar(Id = Guid.NewGuid(), Name = "test3") |]
    |> Queryable.AsQueryable
    |> Repository.get

let context = { new Object()
                    interface IDisposable with
                        member x.Dispose() = () }

let a_GuitarController = new GuitarsController(context, fakeRepository)

let getting_all_guitars (c:GuitarsController) = c.Get()

[<Scenario>]
let ``When getting all the guitars from the repository``() =
  Given a_GuitarController
    |> When getting_all_guitars
    |> It should have (length 3)
    |> It should contain expectedGuitar
    |> Verify
```

In this example, the GuitarsController is instantiated and passed to the function getting_all_guitars. That output is then passed to each assertion function. Lastly, all are verified.

NaturalSpec provides several options for arranging your tests and includes functions that give you options to improve test readability. It also includes an object mocking framework for scenarios where object expressions aren't enough. This is especially useful when using NaturalSpec to test traditional object-oriented code.

 NaturalSpec also requires the binding redirects I have mentioned a few times in this chapter. It should be noted that NUnit will not pick up the config file unless it follows a specific naming convention (*http:// nunit.org/?p=configFiles&r=2.5.3*). I've found that the instructions associated with the single AppDomain scenario work the best.

Summary

Throughout this chapter you have seen various ways to create and test services with F#. These services can be written with different frameworks to solve a wide variety of problems. No matter which option fits your scenario, the unique features of F# are sure to improve that experience.

In the next chapter, we will look at F# combined with Windows Azure. I'll show you how you can use this combination to create more robust, scalable solutions and how you can use the knowledge you've already gained to build F# apps for the cloud. Additionally, I will continue to bring your attention to F# features as well as tools, frameworks, and techniques that can make your life easier. Onward and upward!

CHAPTER 3

To the Cloud! Taking Advantage of Azure

The future is here, it's just not evenly
distributed yet.

—William Gibson

The Preface of this book mentioned that technology is consistently trending towards economies of scale combined with efficient, scalable, and highly available solutions that are intended to be consumable from any modern computing device the user might be utilizing at the time. When it comes to achieving this goal, Windows Azure is a major enabler. The cloud is the future, and platforms such as Windows Azure are helping to evenly distribute it.

It's easy to see the appeal of Windows Azure. The start-up and operational costs are less than they are with on-premises setups, you no longer have to worry about hardware upkeep, and you can reuse much of your existing development knowledge. That being said, there are a few differences that you must consider when architecting and building solutions for the cloud. Most notably, you must design for scaling across a quantity of commodity servers (i.e., scaling out) rather than seeking to build for environments that primarily scale up. F# is perfect for building this type of solution.

In this chapter I'll walk you through creating and deploying F# solutions for the cloud. I'll also show you how to communicate with other roles in your solution and how to harness several of the features that Windows Azure provides. Lastly, I'll showcase a few of the great F# libraries and frameworks that have been built specifically to take advantage of Windows Azure.

Before we dive in, there are a couple of other things I need to say about this chapter. First, it is strongly recommended that you review the "how to" guides provided online (*http://www.windowsazure.com/en-us/develop/net/*) for interacting with Windows Azure through the Windows Azure SDK for .NET. Rather than duplicating in this chapter all of the content from these online guides, I have chosen to provide only highlights from these guides as well as F#-specific implementation details. If you wish to learn more about Windows Azure than what is provided in this chapter and in the online "how to" guides, I recommend reading *Programming Windows Azure* by Sriram Krishnan (O'Reilly).

The second important thing to point out is that this chapter takes a slightly different approach than the preceding two chapters. The first several sections of this chapter introduce a number of concepts and approaches for interacting with Windows Azure. While code samples are provided for demonstration purposes, the examples are fairly abstract. If you prefer slightly more real-world examples, never fear. "Building for Scalability" (page 86) provides a more real-world example that applies several of the abstract code aspects presented prior to that point while also showcasing a helpful approach for building applications that scale well in Windows Azure.

Building and Hosting F# on Azure

Windows Azure offers excellent tooling to help you build and deploy your applications to the Web. To get started, simply download and install the Windows Azure SDK for .NET from the Windows Azure .NET Developer Center (*https://www.windowsazure.com/en-us/develop/net/*).

 Support for the Windows Azure SDK for .NET on Visual Studio 2012 RC was released in June 2012. The examples in this book have been tested with this release.

As I mentioned previously, you can reuse everything you've already learned in this book when building solutions for Windows Azure. For example, to build and host the solution that is generated from the F#/C# ASP.NET Web API project template that we looked at in Chapter 2 you only have to follow a few steps:

1. Run Visual Studio as an Administrator.

2. Create an F#/C# ASP.NET Web API solution from the installed templates under Visual F#→ASP.NET→F# and C# Web Application (ASP.NET MVC 4).

3. Add a new Windows Azure Project to the solution from the installed templates under Visual C#→Cloud→Windows Azure Cloud Service. Click OK when presented with subproject options.

 You may be tempted to select the ASP.NET MVC 4 Web Role when shown the Windows Azure Project Creation Wizard; however, this should be avoided.

4. Lastly, right-click on the Roles folder in the new cloud project and add the web app by selecting "Web Role Project in solution…"

That's it. The Solution Explorer should now look something like Figure 3-1. You can now run the solution locally using the Windows Azure Compute Emulator.

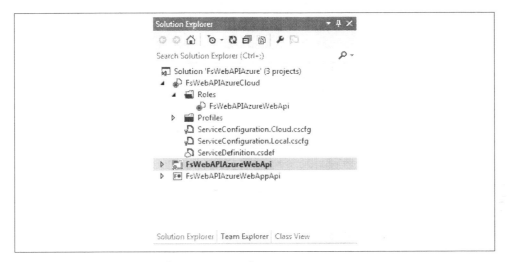

Figure 3-1. F# ASP.NET Web API Azure solution

 If you do not have SQL Express installed on your development box you will receive an error when attempting to run the solution locally indicating that the Development Storage failed to initialize. To fix this, you need to tell the storage emulator what DB instance should be used instead. You can do this by launching the Windows Azure command prompt and typing `DSInit /sqlinstance:<instance name>` (e.g., `DSInit /sqlinstance:SQL2K8`).

You can now push this solution to the cloud by following the instructions in the "Deploy the Application to Windows Azure" section on the online Windows Azure tutorial (*http://bit.ly/windows-azure*). As I mentioned in the introduction to this chapter, I often do not repeat the information provided in the various online tutorials, so if deploying an application to Windows Azure is new to you, I strongly encourage you to walk through the online tutorial.

Creating an F# Worker Role

Creating an F# worker role is even easier than creating a web role. This is largely due to the F# worker role template, which was originally provided as a separate download but is now included with the Windows Azure Tools for Microsoft Visual Studio (part of the previously mentioned SDK). All you have to do is to add a new Windows Azure Project to the solution from the installed templates under Visual C#→Cloud→Windows Azure Cloud Service, double-click the Visual F# Worker Role in the resultant New Windows Azure Project Creation Wizard, optionally change the name of the worker role project, and click OK. Figure 3-2 shows the Windows Azure Project Creation Wizard after selecting the F# Worker Role and changing the project name.

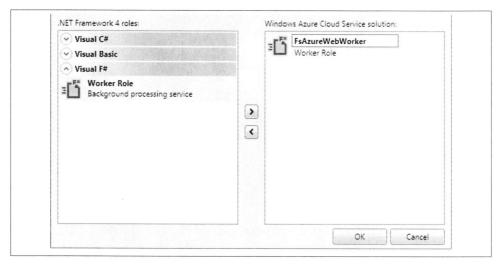

Figure 3-2. Windows Azure Project Creation Wizard after selecting the F# Worker Role and changing the project name

Introducing Fog

Windows Azure provides its API through HTTP services. This is advantageous as it allows any programming language to interact with the platform. Additionally, various wrappers have been created to allow interaction from specific languages to be even easier. If you're creating a .NET application, the easiest option is to use the Windows Azure SDK for .NET, which I mentioned earlier.

While the SDK for .NET can be used from F# in much the same way as from C# or VB.NET, it's certainly geared for more of an object-oriented paradigm. In order to take advantage of some of the unique features of F#, I have created a library called Fog.

Fog brings the cloud down to Earth and harnesses it with F#. Its goal is to reduce boilerplate code as well as to provide a more functional way of interacting with Windows

Azure. Throughout the rest of this chapter I will show you some of the code you could use to interact with Azure without Fog, as well as some of the ways Fog makes your life easier. You can find Fog on my GitHub (*https://github.com/dmohl/Fog*) and get it from NuGet as package ID `Fog`.

Interacting with Azure Storage Options

Windows Azure provides a few different options when it comes to data storage. You'll likely use table storage and SQL Azure for transactional needs and Blob storage for the housing of large data such as files. Depending on your needs, you may also use queue storage.

In this section I'll talk about storing and retrieving data from these storage options using F# and the Windows Azure .NET API. Additionally, I'll show you how to use Fog to improve this experience.

Blobs

Blobs are the primary storage option for larger data types. A single Blob storage account can hold just about anything less than 100 TB in size. Blob storage can be separated into logical containers and is often used to store unstructured data such as images, video, audio, and other files. The Windows Azure website (*http://bit.ly/blob-storage*) provides an excellent tutorial for getting up and running with Blob storage.

From an F# perspective, you could pretty much directly port the C# examples from the Windows Azure Blob storage tutorial into an F# web or worker role and call it a day. Here's an example of how you could call the API to create a blob:

```
let storageAccount =
    RoleEnvironment.GetConfigurationSettingValue "BlobStorageConnectionString"
    |> CloudStorageAccount.Parse

let client = storageAccount.CreateCloudBlobClient()
let container = client.GetContainerReference("testcontainer")
container.CreateIfNotExist() |> ignore

let blob = GetBlobReferenceInContainer container "testblob"
blob.UploadText "My super awesome text to upload"
```

To interact with Blob storage with Fog, install the `Fog` NuGet package into an Azure web or worker role. Next, add a Blob storage connection string with a name `BlobStorage ConnectionString`. You can now upload a blob with a single line of code such as this:

```
UploadBlob "testcontainer" "testblob" "My super awesome text to upload"
```

To retrieve that blob, use code such as the following:

```
DownloadBlob<string> "testcontainer" "testblob"
```

You can also delete blobs, delete containers, and get/set the blob metadata. If the default settings aren't enough for you, Fog provides functions that map more closely to the provided Windows Azure SDK for .NET methods. This allows as much fine-grained control as you require. For example, to retrieve a blob with the same level of control as what was shown in the straight C# port, but with a more succinct syntax, you can do the following:

```
let container = GetBlobContainer <| BuildBlobClient() <| "testcontainer"
UploadBlobToContainer container "testblob" "This is a test"
```

Perhaps you want to use a different connection string name. You can do that with the following code:

```
let container = GetBlobContainer
                <| BuildBlobClientWithConnStr "SomeOtherConnStr"
                <| "testcontainer"
UploadBlobToContainer container "testblob" "This is a test"
```

While I won't go too deep into the implementation details of Fog, I do want to point out various F# features that were really handy while building this library. The first interesting thing to note is how F# can warn you when you're working with classes that implement IDisposable and thus need to be used with use or using. F# doesn't require the new keyword when instantiating classes, and because of this, I often don't use it. However, if the class implements IDisposable, a warning will show up when new isn't used. This becomes a great indicator and reminder that you should use use or using as well as the new keyword for that instance. While building Fog, this F# feature quickly pointed out the scenarios where disposal was needed.

Second, pattern matching with type test patterns was very useful during the creation of the upload and download blob functionality. The Windows Azure SDK for .NET has different methods to accommodate uploads and downloads of different types. Type test patterns allowed me to create a single function to handle most of the different supported types. The match expression for the upload function looks like this:

```
match box item with
| :? Stream as s -> blob.UploadFromStream s
| :? string as text -> blob.UploadText text
| :? (byte[]) as b -> blob.UploadByteArray b
| _ -> failwith "This type is not supported"
```

Tables

Azure table storage is a nonrelational data store for housing structured or semi-structured data. Table storage is an excellent solution for storing transactional data in a format that can quickly be retrieved and displayed on a site. One common approach is to use table storage to hold denormalized representations of data to display on your site or in reports.

Table storage is considered to be a NoSQL data store somewhat similar to Couchbase, CouchDB, MongoDB, RavenDB, and so on. One big difference is that Azure table storage is immediately consistent rather than eventually consistent. Many of the NoSQL options follow an eventually consistent approach, which causes only one of the nodes to be updated before considering the operation a success. This makes the process faster, but can potentially cause reads from different nodes to not always return the most recent data. Azure table storage ensures consistency between nodes before considering the save operation a success. This makes the save operation a little slower, but guarantees immediate consistency.

Interacting with Azure table storage from Fog is easiest when a connection string config entry with the name of `TableStorageConnectionString` is used. Once it is in place, you can use code to add, update, and delete entities from Azure table storage:

```
[<DataServiceKey("PartitionKey", "RowKey")>]
type TestClass() =
    let mutable partitionKey = ""
    let mutable rowKey = ""
    let mutable name = ""
    member x.PartitionKey with get() = partitionKey and set v = partitionKey <- v
    member x.RowKey with get() = rowKey and set v = rowKey <- v
    member x.Name with get() = name and set v = name <- v

let originalClass =
    TestClass(PartitionKey = "TestPart",
                RowKey = Guid.NewGuid().ToString(),
                Name = "test" )

CreateEntity "testtable" originalClass |> ignore

let newClass = originalClass
newClass.Name <- "test2"

UpdateEntity "testtable" newClass |> ignore

DeleteEntity "testtable" newClass
```

 Except where noted, the configuration options for Fog should be placed in the environment-specific *.cscfg files that are found in the Azure project of the solution.

One thing to point out is the use of the `DataServiceKey` attribute and the properties named `PartitionKey` and `RowKey` that are defined in the class that is acting as our entity. These are required when interacting with Windows Azure table storage via the Windows Azure SDK for .NET. To achieve the same effect, you could instead have `TestClass` inherit from `TableStorageEntity`.

Now that the Windows Azure development tools are supported in Visual Studio 2012, you can use the query computation expression that came out with F# 3.0 that was discussed in Chapter 1. If you are using Visual Studio 2010, the best way to query Azure table storage from F# is to use the LINQ support in the F# PowerPack. After installing the `FSPowerPack.Linq.Community` NuGet package and opening `Microsoft.FSharp.Linq.Query`, you can use code such as this to retrieve a specific entity:

```
query <@ seq { for e in context.CreateQuery<TestRecord>("testtable") do
               if e.PartitionKey = testRecord.PartitionKey &&
                  e.RowKey = testRecord.RowKey then
               yield e } @> |> Seq.head
```

Queue Storage

Queue storage isn't used as often now that the Azure Service Bus is available, but it still has a few features that cause it to be useful for certain situations. The most prominent of these is a need to hold a total number of messages that have a combined size greater than 5 GB. The MSDN Library (*http://msdn.microsoft.com/en-us/library/hh767287(VS.103).aspx*) has a complete list of scenarios where queue storage should be used instead of Azure Service Bus.

Fog makes using Azure storage queues as easy as any of the previously mentioned storage options. Simply add a connection string with a name of `QueueStorageConnectionString` and then use code such as the following to add, consume, and/or delete a message:

```
AddMessage "testqueue" "This is a test message" |> ignore
let result = GetMessages "testqueue" 20 5
for m in result do
    DeleteMessage "testqueue" m
```

One functional technique that was used in Fog's queue storage interaction implementation, as well as several other places within Fog, is something known as *memoization*. Memoization is often used as a caching technique to allow a function to only be executed once. Fog uses a `memoize` function similar to the one described by Don Syme (*http://blogs.msdn.com/b/dsyme/archive/2007/05/31/a-sample-of-the-memoization-pattern-in-f.aspx*) to implement this technique. One example of how this is used is shown in the code that follows:

```
memoize (fun conn ->
            let storageAccount = GetStorageAccount conn
            storageAccount.CreateCloudQueueClient() ) connectionString
```

This code creates the cloud queue client for use by all of the other Azure queue-related functions in Fog. By using `memoize`, the creation only occurs once and all other requests simply return the result from the first time the function was run.

SQL Azure

SQL Azure provides a cloud-based SQL instance with much of the same MS SQL functionality you are probably very familiar with from years of on-premises use. Interacting with SQL Azure from F# is not very different from interacting with MS SQL from F#. Because of this, I won't spend much time on this subject other than to point out a few online examples.

There are several options for interacting with MS SQL from F#. For a specific SQL Azure example, check out Matthew Moloney's post (*http://blog.moloneymb.com/?p=206*). Tomas Petricek has a nice post (*http://tomasp.net/blog/dynamic-sql.aspx*) on reading data from a SQL database. Mauricio Scheffer has a great library called FsSql that provides a functional wrapper around ADO.NET. The FsSql GitHub site is available here (*https:// github.com/mausch/FsSql*). There are many more options for interacting with MS SQL from F#, including those that I showed in Chapters 1 and 2. Later in this chapter I will show an example of interacting with SQL Azure with Entity Framework 5.

Taking Advantage of the Azure Service Bus

The Windows Azure Service Bus provides a convenient way to communicate between nodes, roles, and/or applications in a widely distributed solution that requires scalability and high availability. Although the Windows Azure Service Bus also provides relayed messaging, I will concentrate on the brokered messaging functionality in this section. Information on the Service Bus relay functionality is available here (*http://bit.ly/bus-relay*).

Queues

Queues in the Windows Azure Service Bus are somewhat similar to the queues I talked about in "Queue Storage" (page 80). However, the queues provided in the Service Bus are better suited for the majority of scenarios that require a service bus. As I mentioned previously, the MSDN page (*http://msdn.microsoft.com/en-us/library/hh767287(VS. 103).aspx*) that compares and contrasts these two technologies provides all the information you will need to determine which option is right for your specific scenario.

As has been the trend throughout this chapter, one of the easiest ways to use Azure Service Bus queues from F# is via Fog. The recommended configuration settings that allow easier use of Fog with the Azure Service Bus are highlighted in Table 3-1.

Table 3-1. Azure Service Bus configuration settings for Fog

Configuration Setting Name	Description
ServiceBusIssuer	This is associated with the Default Issuer value that can be retrieved by following the instructions in the "Obtain the Default Management Credentials for the Namespace" section of the Windows Azure web page on Service Bus queues (*http://bit.ly/bus-relay*).
ServiceBusKey	This needs to be associated with the Default Key value, which can be found in the same place as the value for the Default Issuer.
ServiceBusScheme	The value associated with this name is the first argument provided to the `CreateServiceUri` method.
ServiceBusNamespace	This should be associated with the value of the namespace that was specified in step 4 of the "Create a Service Namespace" section of the Windows Azure web page on Service Bus queues (*http://bit.ly/bus-relay*).
ServiceBusServicePath	The value associated with this name will be appended to the end of the URI. It's useful in a relay scenario to specify a service operation. For brokered messaging scenarios, this value can be blank.

Topics

Topics allow publish/subscribe architectures, where one or more publishers push out messages that can be consumed by one or more subscribers. When a subscription to a topic is made, something similar to a virtual queue is created for that subscriber so that it will have its own copy of the published message for processing. Any other subscribers of the topic will also get their own copy of the message. This can be really useful in a variety of scenarios.

As an example, one common approach in solutions that use NoSQL data stores is to have a denormalized version (or versions) of the data in the NoSQL store as well as a normalized version of the data in an SQL store. This allows you to achieve excellent performance on the NoSQL side, while utilizing features provided by SQL that are best suited for things such as ad hoc reporting and data mining.

You could solve this by publishing a single message that is picked up by a process and pushed to each data store in a serial manner. However, the performance of this approach wouldn't be all that great, since the operation would have to wait for each data save to complete. If you were to then add additional data stores (e.g., a data warehouse, etc.), that serial save operation would increase in runtime yet again. Additionally, adding new data stores would require modifications to that single consumer process that is pushing the requests to the data stores. This would make for a tightly coupled solution that not only doesn't scale well, but also isn't very extensible.

With a publish/subscribe (a.k.a. pub/sub) model, worker roles that are responsible for updating each data store could subscribe to a specific topic. One or more publishers could then push messages containing the new data to a desired topic. Each subscriber of the topic would then receive its copy of the message and update the data store for which it is respectively responsible. Combine this with asynchronous calls and you have a decoupled, fast solution that scales by simply adding more commodity servers. In "Building for Scalability" (page 86), I will provide an example of this approach. For now, we must learn the basics of how to interact with Azure Service Bus topics.

The easiest way to use Fog with Azure Service Bus topics is to first add the config settings I mentioned in "Queues" (page 81) and then add code such as the following:

```
type TestRecord = { Name : string }
let testRecord = { Name = "test" }

Subscribe "topictest" "AllTopics1"
    <| fun m -> printfn "%s" m.GetBody<TestRecord>().Name
    <| fun ex m -> raise ex

Subscribe "topictest" "AllTopics2"
    <| fun m -> printfn "%s" m.GetBody<TestRecord>().Name
    <| fun ex m -> raise ex

Publish "topictest2" testRecord
```

The emphasized code creates two subscribers, one named `AllTopics1` and one named `AllTopics2`. These are each subscribing to the `topictest` topic. The record instance named `testRecord` is then sent as a message to the `topictest` topic, which will cause the two subscribers to each receive the message.

Unsubscribing from a topic is as easy as:

```
Unsubscribe "topictest" "AllTopics1"
```

Removing a topic is also done with a single call, as shown in the next example. It should be mentioned that the majority of the functions in Fog have checks in place to create before attempting to delete (if the target of the delete doesn't exist for some reason). This means that calling `DeleteTopic` with a topic name that doesn't exist will result in the creation of the topic followed by the immediate deletion of that topic:

```
DeleteTopic "topictest"
```

Exploring Authentication and Authorization

Windows Azure includes a few options when it comes to authentication and authorization. While you can host a site that uses a Membership Provider approach in Azure (with the help of the ASP.NET Universal Providers, which can be found on NuGet as ID `System.Web.Providers`), the trend in the security space has steadily been migrating to standards-based protocols such as SAML and OAuth that allow federated single sign-on. While these protocols are a huge step in the right direction, they are known for being difficult to get set up.

Azure makes this setup into a somewhat trivial afterthought with the help of the *Access Control Service* (ACS). With just a few clicks in the Azure Management Portal, you can have your site configured to accept security tokens from a few of the major identity providers such as Google, Yahoo!, and Windows Live. The Windows Azure Access Control Service web page (*http://bit.ly/bus-queues*) provides steps for how to do this.

With only a little more work you can add a custom identity provider such as an Active Directory Federation Services (ADFS) 2.0 instance that is able to authenticate users from within the Active Directory forest of your organization. Steps for accomplishing this are available here (*http://bit.ly/aspnet-training*).

This particular subject is vast and a few books have already been written on it, so I won't spend too much time going into extensive detail in this book. Instead, I'll explain just a few key concepts and show a couple of ways to work with Windows Identity Foundation —a key component used in .NET to help facilitate federated authentication and authorization—from F#. More information on claims-based authentication and authorization is available here (*http://msdn.microsoft.com/en-us/library/ff423674.aspx*).

Authentication and Authorization with ACS

While often mentioned together, authentication and authorization are two distinct things. *Authentication* is the act of determining the identity of a user. *Authorization* is the act of determining whether the user has access to a specific resource. This could be anything from a whole site to a web page to a specific operation.

ACS can help you achieve both authentication and authorization. Alternatively, it can be used to handle only the authentication, leaving authorization up to your application. Lastly, a hybrid approach can be used in which ACS handles authentication and pieces of authorization, while your application handles more fine-grained authorization. Let's look deeper into authentication and authorization by diving into a few F# examples.

Claims-based Authentication

If you followed the instructions on authenticating web users with ACS (*https:// www.windowsazure.com/en-us/develop/net/how-to-guides/access-control/*), you should be all set up to use Windows Live, Google, and/or Yahoo! for authentication purposes. The primary changes required to use this guide to set up your F# web app are to add the reference to `Microsoft.IdentityModel` and use code similar to the following to create a string representation of all the claim types and associated values:

```
let claimsIdentity = Thread.CurrentPrincipal.Identity :?> ClaimsIdentity
this.ViewData["Claims"] <-
    claimsIdentity.Claims
    |> Seq.fold(
        fun acc c -> acc +
                    sprintf "Type: %s - Value: %s\r\n" c.ClaimType c.Value) ""
```

While this claim-related information isn't something you will likely show to an end user, it can be very valuable to an administrator. To display these results, you can modify the view with code such as this:

```
<pre>@ViewData["Claims"]</pre>
```

In this example, I added the code to the `HomeController` of the ASP.NET Web API Azure solution that I walked you through in "Building and Hosting F# on Azure" (page 74). This code gets the `Identity` of the user and casts it to a `ClaimsIdentity`, which makes it easy for us to grab the details of the claims that make up the security token. The code then uses `Seq.fold` to create a single string that can be displayed on the page to showcase each claim type and value.

If you're not familiar with `Seq.fold`, it might be a little confusing at first. `Seq.fold` takes a collection and loops through it, adding a value to an accumulator (often abbreviated to `acc`) during each iteration, and ultimately results in a single representation of that accumulator. In this example, the collection of claims is being provided to `Seq.fold`. For each iteration, the accumulator (which is a string in this case) and the current claim object are being acted on. The string representation of the claim type and claim value is added to the end of the accumulator, and once all the claims have been cycled through a final string representation of the accumulator is returned. The two double quotes at the end of `Seq.fold` specify the initial value of the accumulator. You may remember that we accomplished similar functionality with a slightly different syntax in Chapter 2 by using `Seq.reduce`.

Claims-based Authorization

For authorization purposes, you have a few different options. You can use an approach similar to what I showed in the preceding section and grant or deny access based on the value and/or existence of a specific claim. For example, if I wanted to only display the claims data, which was added to the site in the preceding subsection, when the user has a Gmail address I might use the following code:

```
let claimsIdentity = Thread.CurrentPrincipal.Identity :?> ClaimsIdentity

claimsIdentity.Claims
|> Seq.filter(fun c -> c.ClaimType = ClaimTypes.Email)
|> Seq.map(fun c -> c.Value)
|> Seq.head
|> function
   | v when v.Contains("@gmail.com") ->
       this.ViewData.["Claims"] <-
           claimsIdentity.Claims
           |> Seq.fold(
               fun acc c -> acc +
                       sprintf "Type: %s - Value: %s\r\n"
                           c.ClaimType c.Value) ""
   | _ -> ()
```

The emphasized code in this example gets the sequence of claims and filters it down to only those with an email claim type. It then transforms the sequence of claims into a new sequence that contains only the `Value` from each `Claim`. Next it returns the first result from that sequence and does a pattern match to determine whether the `Value` contains `@gmail.com`.

 If some of the higher-order functions from the Seq module are new and your background is in C#, it's easiest to think of `Seq.filter` as similar to `Enumerable.Where`, `Seq.map` as `Enumerable.Select`, `Seq.head` as `Enumerable.First`, and `Seq.fold` as `Enumerable.Aggregate`.

A second approach is to use the conventions built into *Windows Identity Foundation* (WIF) to transform specific `Claims` into roles. This opens up typical authorization methods such as `IsInRole`. By default, WIF does this by checking for claims with a type of *http://schemas.microsoft.com/ws/2008/06/identity/claims/role*. In the ASP.NET MVC and ASP.NET Web API world, this approach also opens up the `Authorize` attribute as well as libraries such as Fluent Security (*http://www.fluentsecurity.net/getting-started*), or on NuGet as package ID `FluentSecurity`.

Building for Scalability

By now I'm sure you have already identified several advantages of using Azure as it relates to building scalable solutions. The primary thing to keep in mind when building solutions for Azure is to architect for horizontal scalability rather than vertical scalability. This means you will need to build solutions that are distributed across many different machines, all working toward a common goal. Many of the features of F# that we have already discussed will help you accomplish this goal more easily.

In this section, I will walk you through building a simple solution for placing orders for hacky sacks. The solution will be built with one web role and two worker roles. We'll use a few of the features of Azure that we already covered, such as queues, table storage, and SQL Azure. This will provide an example of one approach for building a solution that scales horizontally.

Building the Web Role

For this example we will create a single web role that has a simple user interface consisting of an input box that allows specification of the number of hacky sacks a user wishes to order and a submit button labeled Place Orders. We'll use the form functionality provided by jQuery Mobile combined with the F#/C# ASP.NET Web API template. When the submit button is clicked the system will publish messages to a topic named `Orders`. The order form is shown in Figure 3-3. This is obviously a contrived example since a true order form would include a lot more information, such as who is making the order, where it should be sent, and the method of payment. However, it provides enough information for you to easily use this as a foundation on which to build more complicated solutions.

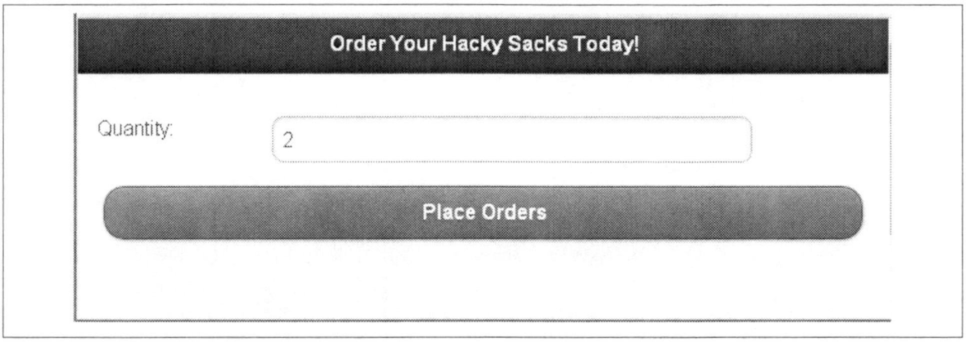

Figure 3-3. Hacky sack order form

To accomplish all of this, I first create an F#/C# ASP.NET MVC 4 Web API solution as defined in "Building and Hosting F# on Azure" (page 74). This web solution will be the sole publisher of messages that are to be consumed and processed by the worker roles. We'll use Fog to publish the messages, so we can now install the Fog NuGet package. To simulate load, the web role will push a single message into the queue for each hacky sack that is purchased.

I next add some JavaScript code. While this code is minimal, the example is a little closer to what I would do in a production app. Specifically, I've used RequireJS and included a module to contain the needed JavaScript. Since the focus of this book is primarily on F#, I will not show this code. However, you can find it here (*http://bit.ly/hacky-sack*).

The JavaScript code does a POST to the appropriate HTTP service provided by ASP.NET Web API. While this functionality could just as easily have been provided with a standard ASP.NET MVC application, I often prefer to provide an HTTP service. This makes it very easy for other solutions to interact with the service. Additionally, if I were to choose to later deploy the client-side code as a native app with a wrapper such as PhoneGap, the use of ASP.NET Web API would help in the transition.

All that the ASP.NET Web API controller needs to do is publish a message with the order information to the Orders topic. This is accomplished by adding the needed config entries to use the service bus functionality built into Fog, changing the ValuesControl ler to be named OrdersController, and adding code such as the following:

```
namespace FsWeb.Controllers

open System
```

```
open System.Web.Http
open FsWeb.Models
open FsWeb.Commands

type OrdersController() =
    inherit ApiController()
    member x.Post (order:HackySackOrder) =
        [1..order.Quantity]
        |> Seq.iter(
            fun i ->
                { RowKey = Guid.NewGuid().ToString()
                  PartitionKey = "Orders"
                  PlacementDateTime = DateTime.Now
                  Quantity = order.Quantity
                  Instance = i }
                |> Fog.ServiceBus.Publish "Orders" )
```

The HackySackOrder class that is expected as input to the Post method looks like this:

```
type HackySackOrder() =
    let mutable quantity = 0
    member x.Quantity with get() = quantity and set v = quantity <- v
```

Understanding the PlaceOrderCommand

You may have noticed that I am creating an instance of a specific record in the Post method of the OrdersController that is then published to the topic. This record is named PlaceOrderCommand. The worker roles will need to be able to deserialize the messages they get from the Service Bus into this record type, so I've placed the Place OrderCommand type in a new project called Commands. The PlaceOrderCommand is going to be persisted in both table storage and SQL Azure. As I mentioned in "Tables" (page 78), table storage requires a few specifically named properties, so I've added RowKey and PartitionKey to the PlaceOrderCommand type. This is an example of how to use an F# record with table storage rather than the approach shown in "Tables" (page 78) that used a class. The PlaceOrderCommand record is shown in the following snippet:

```
namespace FsWeb.Commands

open System
open System.ServiceModel
open System.Runtime.Serialization
open System.Data.Services.Common
open System.ComponentModel.DataAnnotations

[<DataContract>]
[<DataServiceKey("PartitionKey", "RowKey")>]
type PlaceOrderCommand =
    { [<DataMember>] mutable PartitionKey : string
```

```
[<DataMember>] [<Key>] mutable RowKey : string
[<DataMember>] mutable PlacementDateTime : DateTime
[<DataMember>] mutable Quantity : int
[<DataMember>] mutable Instance : int }
```

 As I mentioned a few times in this book, F# 3.0 provides an attribute named CLIMutable that simplifies this example by allowing you to not have to use the mutable keyword for the PlaceOrderCommand record. I'll provide examples and additional explanation of the CLIMutable attribute in Chapter 4.

On to the Worker Roles

The worker roles are responsible for the "real" work of placing the hacky sack order requests in both the SQL Azure and table storage data stores. To showcase different scalability options provided by Azure, we'll provide one instance of the worker role that will interact with SQL and two instances of the worker role that will interact with table storage. The two worker roles that will add the various hacky sack order requests to table storage will compete for messages that are waiting to be processed (this is known as the competing consumer pattern).

To set this up I add two F# worker roles to the solution that was generated in "Building the Web Role" (page 86), one named OrderProcessor2 and one named OrderSQL. Since I want to have two instances of the OrderProcessor2 worker role, I open the *Service Configuration.*.cscfg* file (which can be found in the Windows Azure project of the solution) and change the instances count setting from 1 to 2. Lastly, I install the Fog NuGet package in these new F# projects.

 The *ServiceConfiguration.*.cscfg* file will contain elements for all the projects in the solution. Make sure you change the instances count for only the OrderProcessor2 project.

Now that all the projects are set up, we can add the code needed to interact with table storage. As I previously mentioned, the order processing worker role (named Order Processor2) will be responsible for accomplishing this. While a real-world implementation would contain additional logic such as credit card processing, fulfillment-related tasks, email notifications, and more, the storage mechanism would largely stay the same. I first add the table storage configuration entry needed by Fog to the *ServiceConfiguration.Local.cscfg* file in the Azure project. This specific configuration entry looks like the following:

```
<Setting name="TableStorageConnectionString"
    value="UseDevelopmentStorage=true" />
```

The `OrderProcessor2 WorkerRole` class with the code to subscribe to the `Orders` topic and save the result to table storage ends up looking like this:

```
type WorkerRole() =
    inherit RoleEntryPoint()

    let log message kind = Trace.WriteLine(message, kind)

    override wr.Run() =
        log "OrderProcessor2 entry point called" "Information"
        try
            Fog.ServiceBus.Subscribe "Orders" "OrderProcessor"
                <| fun m ->
                    let entity = m.GetBody<PlaceOrderCommand>()
                    Fog.Storage.Table.CreateEntity "HackySackOrders" entity
                <| fun ex m -> log ex.Message "Error"
        with
        | ex ->
            log ex.Message "Error"

        while(true) do
            Thread.Sleep(10000)

    override wr.OnStart() =
        // Set the maximum number of concurrent connections
        ServicePointManager.DefaultConnectionLimit <- 12
        // For information on handling configuration changes
        // see the MSDN topic at http://go.microsoft.com/fwlink/?LinkId=166357.
        base.OnStart()
```

This code is pretty simple since the messages that are coming in from the Service Bus are already set to persist to table storage. All we do is set up a subscription to the `Orders` topic with a name of `OrderProcessor` and provide functions to handle success and failure scenarios. On success, the body of the message is persisted to table storage.

It's important to use code similar to the `while` loop, which is emphasized in the example. Without something like this, the worker will run the code above it to set up the subscription and then stop running. This would then cause the worker roles to never receive messages.

Wrapping Up the SQL Azure Worker Role

We have now set up our two instances of the worker role that will handle the interaction with table storage, so it's time to add the code for the worker role that will interact with SQL Azure (named `OrderSQLStore`). The `OrderSQLStore` worker uses Entity Framework 5 with a code-first approach. After getting everything set up on the SQL Azure account end of things as well as setting up the configs, the code ends up looking like a combination of our code-first example from Chapter 1 and the subscription code from the `OrdersProcessor2` worker. The example that follows shows the majority of the Entity Framework–related code. The only real difference between this code and that from the example in Chapter 1 is how the connection string information is being picked up and passed to `DbContext`. The example from Chapter 1 provided the name of the connection string to retrieve from the config file. For Azure, we don't have this option, so we add a standard config setting and use `RoleEnvironment.GetConfiguration SettingValue` to retrieve it and provide it to `DbContext`:

```
namespace FsWeb.Repositories

open Microsoft.WindowsAzure.ServiceRuntime
open System.Data.Entity
open FsWeb.Commands

type HackySackStoreEntities() =
    inherit DbContext(
        RoleEnvironment.GetConfigurationSettingValue
        <| "HackySackStoreConnectionString")

    do Database.SetInitializer(
        CreateDatabaseIfNotExists<HackySackStoreEntities>())

    [<DefaultValue(true)>] val mutable orderCommands : DbSet<PlaceOrderCommand>
    member x.OrderCommands
        with get() = x.orderCommands and set v = x.orderCommands <- v
```

The code to handle messages from the `Orders` topic sets up a subscription named `OrderSQLStore`. Any messages that come in are then passed to a function that will add the entity to the SQL Azure database. Here's the code:

```
let handleNewOrderCommand entity =
    try
        use context = new HackySackStoreEntities()
        context.OrderCommands.Add entity |> ignore
        context.SaveChanges() |> ignore
    with
    | ex ->
        log ex.Message "Error"
        raise ex

override wr.Run() =
    log "OrderSQLStore entry point called" "Information"
    try
        Fog.ServiceBus.Subscribe "Orders" "OrderSQLStore"
            <| fun m ->
                m.GetBody<PlaceOrderCommand>()
                |> handleNewOrderCommand
            <| fun ex m -> log ex.Message "Error"
    with
```

```
    | ex -> log ex.Message "Error"

    while(true) do
        Thread.Sleep(10000)
```

Adding the Finishing Touches

When you run all the roles together you'll find that the records are appropriately making it into both SQL Azure and to table storage. You may have also noticed that the site shows the Ajax spinner for a while longer than what you might like. This is because the Publish function is doing its work synchronously. Since our goal is to create a highly responsive solution, this simply won't do. With the current, synchronous approach, the response time of this one POST with one user will increase simply because more orders are being placed.

There are a few ways to solve this, and as usual F# makes it really easy. All you have to do is to wrap the call to Publish in an async block and kick it off. The updated code with the two new lines emphasized is shown in the following example:

```
type OrdersController() =
    inherit ApiController()
    member x.Post (order:HackySackOrder) =
        [1..order.Quantity]
        |> Seq.iter(
            fun i ->
                async {
                    { RowKey = Guid.NewGuid().ToString()
                      PartitionKey = "Orders"
                      PlacementDateTime = DateTime.Now
                      Quantity = order.Quantity
                      Instance = i }
                    |> Fog.ServiceBus.Publish "Orders"
                } |> Async.Start )
```

Our example is now complete and running well. However, there are a few additional topics that I still want to cover that can help you build scalable solutions.

 The examples shown in the rest of this book are not extensions of this hacky sack orders example. They should be viewed in isolation.

Caching

Along with asynchrony, horizontal scaling, load balancing, and functional approaches such as memorization, caching is an important part of a scalable solution. While caching can easily be done in-process, it loses some of its effectiveness due to size limitations, lack of shared access, and loss of the cache on process restart. This is often resolved by moving the cache out-of-process and into a SQL database, but this has a performance cost.

One solution that offers a return on investment is to use a distributed caching approach. This reduces the size limitations, allows the cache to live through an application pool recycle, and makes the cache available to all desired processes. Additionally, while there is some overhead associated with pushing and pulling data across the wire from the cache cluster, the performance is generally better than storing the cache in SQL. Many of the modern distributed cache solutions also offer local cache configuration options that reduce this overhead even more.

Windows Azure provides distributed caching functionality through a service called… drum roll please…Windows Azure Caching. You can find basic instructions on how to set it up and use it here (*https://www.windowsazure.com/en-us/develop/net/how-to-guides/cache/*). Fog wraps the Azure Caching service API in a module named `Fog.Cach ing`. You can now create an Azure solution with either a web or worker role, install Fog, and use code such as this:

```
let rowKey = Guid.NewGuid().ToString()

{ RowKey = rowKey
  PartitionKey = "Orders"
  PlacementDateTime = DateTime.Now
  Quantity = order.Quantity
  Instance = 1 }
|> Put rowKey |> ignore
```

The emphasized code initializes a `PlaceOrderCommand` record (which was shown in the hacky sack order example) using a record expression and then puts it in the Azure distributed cache. To later retrieve that cached value you can do this:

```
let result = Get<PlaceOrderCommand> rowKey
```

The `Get` function returns an option type, which allows you to easily tell whether the value already exists in cache without fear of a null reference error.

 All of the Azure examples up to this point have used the *.cscfg* files for configuration. Caching is a bit different in that the configuration options are expected to be placed in an app or web config file.

CDN and Autoscaling

There are two last Windows Azure features that I want to talk about in this section. While the F# language doesn't provide any specific benefits for these two features, they can be important in the creation of scalable F# solutions that run on Windows Azure. The first is a *content delivery network* (CDN) and the second is *autoscaling*.

Content delivery networks offer another key cog in the wheel of scalable solution development. Windows Azure allows you to use a CDN to distribute cached versions of blobs stored in Blob storage. This not only provides the benefit of caching your content, but also gets that content closer to the user. The closer the content is to the user, the faster the site is for her.

To use F# to get your data into the Windows Azure CDN, use Fog to push the desired content into Blob storage. You can then follow the directions on the Windows Azure CDN web page (*http://bit.ly/using-cdn*) to set up a new CDN endpoint.

When using some of the techniques we've discussed we can easily scale out by adding more commodity server instances that work together as competing consumers to accomplish the desired goals. Often, solutions built with this pattern in mind must account for the worst-case load scenario plus a healthy contingency. It's cheaper to spend the money on hardware than to lose out on sales or customer confidence due to a system crash caused by unexpected high volumes of users.

Ideally, you could somehow deploy for common usage scenarios and then ramp up or down as needed based on usage or known high-traffic periods. This is exactly what autoscaling gives you. With a number of configuration entries and a few lines of code you can define rules that allow your solution to scale as needed. You can find the steps to set this up here (*http://bit.ly/using-cdn*).

Shining F# Examples

The F# team combined with the F# community have been doing some exciting stuff with F# and Windows Azure. In this section I will point out a few of these shining examples. These libraries and frameworks leverage the power of F# to accomplish things that would be more difficult in a language such as C# or VB.NET.

In addition to the libraries and frameworks provided in this section, there are a few videos and articles available that offer great information and examples of using F# with Azure. For instance, Don Syme (the creator of F#) showcases F# combined with Windows Azure (*http://bit.ly/don-syme*). As another example, Noah Gift provides an excellent walkthrough (*http://bit.ly/parsing-logfiles*) of how to use F# and Azure to parse logfiles.

{m}brace

F# really shines in the area of distributed computing. Language features such as computation expressions and `MailboxProcessor` (a.k.a. agent) open the doors for computing that focuses on message passing concurrency. While the existing features offer a lot of advantages, there is still work to do.

A company named Nessos Information Technologies has built a framework and runtime that makes creating distributed computing solutions with F# trivial. Similar to many of the features provided by Erlang, the framework and runtime (named {m}brace) provides seamless distribution and boasts a number of additional features including hot code swapping, code optimizations, process and dataflow orchestration, extensive logging and tracing, and actor combinators.

As an example of one of the many features, consider the following code that uses a few small pieces of the actor framework provided by {m}brace:

```
type PingPong = | Ping
let rec pingPongBehavior (self: Actor<PingPong>) = async {
    let! message = self.Receive()

    match message with
    | Ping ->
        log
        <| sprintf "Pong received at %O by %s" DateTime.Now self.Name
        <| "Information"

    return! pingPongBehavior self }

let actor1 = Actor.bind "actor1" pingPongBehavior
let actor2 = Actor.bind "actor2" pingPongBehavior
let supervisor = Actor.broadcast [actor1; actor2]

supervisor.Start()

!supervisor <-- Ping
```

The first function, `pingPongBehavior`, isn't all the different from what you might see when creating a `MailboxProcessor` as we did in Chapter 1. It gets more interesting when we get to the definition of `actor1`, `actor2`, and `supervisor`. `actor1` and `actor2` are simply binding a name to an actor instance and associating the `pingPongBehavior` function as the logic for each actor instance. The `supervisor` actor is then set up to send messages to each actor. Under the covers, the `broadcast` function spawns `actor1` and `actor2` as actors linked to `superviser`. This not only allows `supervisor` to broadcast messages to the linked actors, but also allows the `supervisor` agent to control the starting and stopping of these actors.

You can find a few slides and a number of great examples here (*http://bit.ly/m-brace*). Additionally, a recorded presentation is available here (*http://bit.ly/skills-matter*).

Cloud Numerics

The Cloud Numerics library provides support to scale solutions that need to do numerical and/or data analytics on large amounts of data with calculations that require extensive computational power. A lab that includes instructions for getting set up, as well as several examples, is available online (*http://social.technet.microsoft.com/wiki/contents/articles/5993.microsoft-codename-cloud-numerics.aspx*). Additional information is also available on the MSDN Blogs web page (*http://bit.ly/cloud-numerics*).

The library has several features, including numerical and array methods and data structures that work well in a distributed environment, a project template and sample application, and a deployment utility that makes configuring and publishing to a cluster in Azure quite easy.

Framework for .NET Hadoop MapReduce

Hadoop is a framework that is well known in the big data space. It allows distributed processing and querying of large data sets across clusters that scale to massive sizes. Windows Azure now offers Hadoop services. At the time of this writing, the Hadoop services on Azure are in developer preview and only available by invitation. You can request an invitation here (*https://www.hadooponazure.com/*).

In the current implementation, the best way to interact with Hadoop from F# is through Hadoop Streaming. Carl Nolan has put together a great library, along with some F# examples (*http://bit.ly/hadoop-streaming*), that makes writing Hadoop Streaming MapReduce jobs a breeze. Additionally, Carl has several blog posts (*http://blogs.msdn.com/b/carlnol/*) that provide additional information and examples.

Summary

F# and Windows Azure pair up very nicely. As I've shown you throughout this chapter, interacting with Windows Azure through the Windows Azure SDK for .NET and F# is even easier than doing so with C# or VB.NET. With a library such as Fog, that experience becomes trivial. Additionally, frameworks such as {m}brace, Cloud Numerics, and Hadoop Streaming and F# MapReduce allow you to use the power of F# to handle large data sets and/or computationally intensive requirements without breaking a sweat.

In the next chapter we'll dive into additional ways to increase the speed of your F#-based web solutions and allow them to scale to large proportions. I'll walk you through creating web sockets, using SignalR in web and mobile scenarios, storing data with the help of various NoSQL solutions, and more.

CHAPTER 4

Constructing Scalable Web and Mobile Solutions

The most important thing in science is not so much to obtain new facts as to discover new ways of thinking about them.

—Sir William Bragg

If you're like me, it takes very little for you to recall your first experience with a computer. In fact, the act of reading that last sentence probably took you back in your mind's eye to whenever that time was.

I first touched a computer in 1985 when my parents brought home an IBM PC. It was decked out with two 5×7-inch floppy disk drives and a lovely green-screen monitor. I was instantly intrigued and quickly started diving into the several instruction binders that came with this mystical machine so that I could learn the magic that would allow me to harness its power. A few successful lines of BASICA later and I was hooked.

While massive advancements have been made in the area of computers, many of the core concepts have remained the same. These advancements were often made by discovering new ways to think about existing facts. Without these new ways of thinking, we would certainly not be where we are today.

New ways of thinking continue to be developed daily and the constant advances in technology reflect this. Many of these advances have had a positive side effect of causing more and more people to have access to the Internet than ever before. These users of the Web expect sites that are highly responsive and that work with a variety of modern devices. Other advances have shifted the access of the Internet from the traditional stationary locations to mobility. In fact, the CTIA Wireless Association has indicated that there are more wireless subscriber connections in the United States and its territories than people, according to a CNET News article (*http://cnet.co/XdKGBm*).

In order to provide responsive and adaptive solutions that scale to the number of users that are now required, we too must discover new ways to think about various technologies and approaches. I've already shown several ways to help your solutions meet increasing speed and scalability needs. This chapter provides additional approaches and F# examples to further this knowledge.

Scaling with Web Sockets

Web Sockets has been getting a lot of press recently. This highly publicized feature is part of the in-progress HTML5 specification. Though the spec is still in-progress, this hasn't stopped many of the major players from building HTML5 features into their browsers. The feature known as Web Sockets is no exception.

Web Sockets provides a mechanism for two-way communication between the client and the server. This makes your site faster and more scalable by reducing the number of requests and shrinking the payload size of any sent packets. Additionally, the full-duplex communication channel that a web socket provides allows the information on a page to update in near–real time. You can find more information about the benefits of Web Sockets here (*http://www.websocket.org/quantum.html*).

 While Web Sockets can certainly improve the performance and scalability of your site, you should use it responsibly. More information can be found here (*http://bit.ly/html5-sockets*).

You may be wondering what areas of your solution or types of solution would best benefit from the use of Web Sockets. The typical response would be "anything that needs to be updated in real time," but that seems a bit too generic. Here are a few specific ideas that seem to be a great fit: real-time site usage statistics and reporting, stock ticker displays, the canonical chat example, real-time games, a Kanban board, and user alerts and notifications. In practice, you will need to evaluate your solution to determine which pieces require the advantages that Web Sockets provides, and utilize them only in these areas.

Building a Web Socket Example with .NET 4.5 and IIS 8

There are a few options when it comes to building web socket servers. Versions of IIS earlier than IIS 8 do not support Web Sockets. So if you want to host your web socket in IIS, you'll have to use IIS 8 and .NET 4.5. Paul Batum talks more about this and shows a C# example in his blog (*http://www.paulbatum.com/2011/09/getting-started-with-websockets-in.html*). The F# example that follows takes a similar approach as defined in Paul's post.

> There is an unsupported prototype for Web Sockets (*http://bit.ly/ sockets-prototype*) that will work in theory in earlier versions of IIS.

Let's build a simple survey that will provide a charted view of the responses in real time via a web socket. The survey will provide a single question that asks, "What is your favorite programming language?" Possible answers include F#, C#, Erlang, JavaScript, and Other. With a tiny bit of help from the Twitter Bootstrap CSS, the web version of the question aspect of our survey appears as shown in Figure 4-1. The image shows two instances of Chrome side by side, with our survey loaded in each. This will make it easy for us to see how responsive our website becomes when using Web Sockets.

> You will need to run Visual Studio in administrator mode to execute this example.

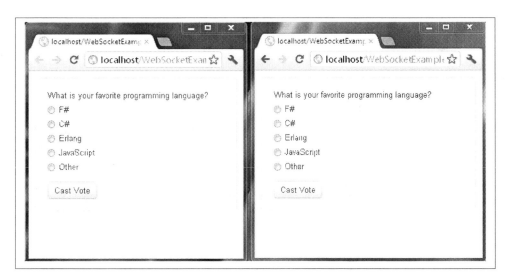

Figure 4-1. Survey form

The view that displays after you have submitted the answer to the survey question shows a chart that represents all responses to the survey. This is the view we want to update in real time. We'll use a JavaScript charting library called D3 (*http://d3js.org/*). Since it's not directly related to the web socket aspects of this example, I won't show the D3-related code. However, you can find it in the *mainModule.js* file in the WebSocketIIS8Example project (*https://github.com/dmohl/fs-web-cloud-mobile/tree/master/Ch%204*).

After enabling web sockets in IIS 8, we create a new ASP.NET MVC 4 application and make sure all projects are set to use .NET 4.5. We can now install the `Microsoft.Web Sockets` NuGet package. We can also add a new *.ashx* file to the C# project and a few supporting *.fs* files to the F# WebApp project.

The first *.fs* file in this example is named *ChartWebSocket.ashx.fs* and it's similar in concept to the code-behind *.cs* file that is often created when an *.ashx* item is created in a C# project. The code in this file creates a class that implements `IHttpHandler`. When a web socket request is processed, a new instance of a `WebSocketChartHandler` class is instantiated. The code looks like this:

```
namespace FsWeb

open System
open System.Web
open Microsoft.Web.WebSockets
open WebSocketServer

type ChartWebSocket() =
    interface IHttpHandler with
        member x.ProcessRequest context =
            if context.IsWebSocketRequest then
                context.AcceptWebSocketRequest(new WebSocketChartHandler())
        member x.IsReusable = true
```

The *WebSocketChartHandler.fs* file is composed of a few different pieces. First a `Web SocketCollection` is created to keep track of all the clients. Second, a `VoteCounts` record is defined. This will be used as the container that later gets serialized to JSON and sent to each web socket client. These two pieces of code look like the following:

```
let mutable clients = WebSocketCollection()

type VoteCounts = { language : string; count : int }
```

To help us out, a `MailboxProcessor` is used to keep a running total of the votes that have been cast for each programming language. This example could easily be extended to store the survey results in a database, but for the sake of simplicity we will be storing the responses in memory. The `MailboxProcessor` implementation looks like this:

```
type Message =
    | Vote of string * AsyncReplyChannel<seq<string*int>>
```

```
let votesAgent = MailboxProcessor.Start(fun inbox ->
    let rec loop votes =
        async {
            let! message = inbox.Receive()
            match message with
            | Vote(language, replyChannel) ->
                let newVotes = language::votes
                newVotes
                |> Seq.countBy(fun lang -> lang)
                |> replyChannel.Reply
                do! loop(newVotes)
            do! loop votes
        }
    loop List.empty)
```

The `MailboxProcessor` implementation isn't all that different from the one shown in Chapter 1, so I will only spend time explaining the code that is emphasized.

When a `Vote` message is received from the virtual queue, it's added to an F# list. F# lists are *singly linked list* data structures, which allow them to perform well while remaining immutable. This list performs well because a copy of the list isn't created each and every time a new value is added. Instead, the new value is added to a new address space and a reference is used to point to the rest of the list. We use the *cons* operator (`::`) to make this happen. After the operation is complete the new survey result will effectively be at the front of the list.

The votes are then counted for each language and a sequence of `string * int` is returned. For example, if three votes for F# have been cast, along with one for C# and two for JavaScript, the result of pushing a new vote for F# into the `MailboxProcessor` would be a sequence that conceptually contains `F#, 4; C#, 1; JavaScript, 2`.

The last bit of code contained in the *WebSocketChartHandler.fs* file is the `WebSocketChartHandler` class definition. This class inherits `WebSocketHandler` and overrides three of the methods it contains. The code looks like this:

```
type WebSocketChartHandler() =
    inherit WebSocketHandler()

    override x.OnOpen() = clients.Add x
    override x.OnMessage(language:string) =
        votesAgent.PostAndReply(fun reply -> Message.Vote(language, reply))
        |> Seq.map(fun v -> { language = fst v; count = snd v } )
        |> JsonConvert.SerializeObject
        |> clients.Broadcast
    override x.OnClose() =
        clients.Remove x |> ignore
```

Each method is pretty self-explanatory, so I'll concentrate on the emphasized code in the `OnMessage` method. The first line sends the vote to the `MailboxProcessor` and waits for the reply. The result of that call is passed to Seq.map to be projected into a sequence of the VoteCounts record that was shown previously. This sequence of VoteCounts is then serialized to JSON using Json.NET. Lastly, the result is broadcast to all clients of the web socket.

The following is an abbreviated version of the JavaScript that connects to the web socket server:

```
$(function () {
    var uri,
        updateChart,
        $pages = $(".page");

    $pages.hide();
    $pages.first().toggle();

    updateChart = function (data) {
        /* Removed for brevity */
    };

    uri = "ws://localhost/WebSocketExample/ChartWebSocket.ashx";

    websocket = new WebSocket(uri);

    websocket.onopen = function () {
        $("#vote").click(function (event) {
            var vote = $("input:radio[name=langOption]:checked");

            if (vote.length) {
                websocket.send(vote.val());
            };

            $pages.hide();
            $("#results").toggle();

            event.preventDefault();
        });
    };

    websocket.onmessage = function (event) {
        updateChart($.parseJSON(event.data));
    };
});
```

You can see this in action by opening two browser instances as shown in Figure 4-1 and casting votes for your favorite language(s). Each browser will show a bar chart that contains the total votes cast for each language that has at least one vote. Additionally, the bar chart on each browser will update to display the latest totals almost immediately after clicking the Cast Vote button from any of the clients. Figure 4-2 shows an example of this.

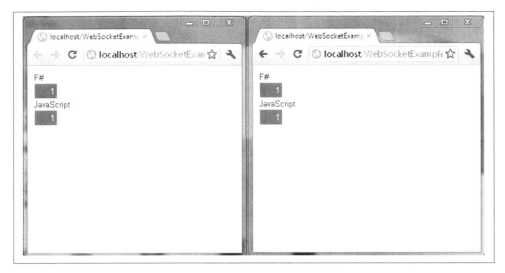

Figure 4-2. Survey results

Creating a Web Socket Server with Fleck

Although the example I just showed works well, what do we do when we don't have IIS 8, don't want to upgrade to .NET 4.5, or want to host the web socket outside of IIS? Luckily, there are several options available to us. My favorite is a library called Fleck. To get started with Fleck, install the `Fleck` NuGet package. You can then use code such as the following to stand up a self-hosted web socket server:

```
module FsFleckServer

open System
open System.Collections.Generic
open Fleck
open Newtonsoft.Json

type VoteCounts = { language : string; count : int }

type Message =
    | Vote of string * AsyncReplyChannel<seq<string*int>>

let votesAgent = MailboxProcessor.Start(fun inbox ->
    let rec loop votes =
        async {
            let! message = inbox.Receive()
            match message with
            | Vote(language, replyChannel) ->
                let newVotes = language::votes
                newVotes
                |> Seq.countBy(fun lang -> lang)
```

```
                    |> replyChannel.Reply
                do! loop(newVotes)
            do! loop votes
        }
    loop List.empty)

let main() =
    FleckLog.Level <- LogLevel.Debug
    let clients = List<IWebSocketConnection>()
    use server = new WebSocketServer "ws://localhost:8181"

    let socketOnOpen socket = clients.Add socket

    let socketOnClose socket = clients.Remove socket |> ignore

    let socketOnMessage language =
        let results =
            votesAgent.PostAndReply(fun reply -> Message.Vote(language, reply))
            |> Seq.map(fun v -> { language = fst v; count = snd v } )
            |> JsonConvert.SerializeObject
        clients |> Seq.iter(fun c -> c.Send results)

    server.Start(fun socket ->
                    socket.OnOpen <- fun () -> socketOnOpen socket
                    socket.OnClose <- fun () -> socketOnClose socket
                    socket.OnMessage <- fun message -> socketOnMessage message)

    Console.ReadLine() |> ignore

main()
```

About the using Function

I've talked about the use keyword a few times now and briefly mentioned the using
function, but haven't provided any examples as of yet that show how to use using. The
using function allows you to have more control over when Dispose() will be called.
Here's how we could have written the code in the main module of the Fleck example
using the using function:

```
using (new WebSocketServer "ws://localhost:8181")
    (fun server ->
        let socketOnOpen socket = clients.Add socket

        let socketOnClose socket = clients.Remove socket |> ignore

        let socketOnMessage language =
            let results =
                votesAgent.PostAndReply(fun reply ->
                                            Message.Vote(language, reply))
                |> Seq.map(fun v -> { language = fst v; count = snd v } )
                |> JsonConvert.SerializeObject
```

```
            clients |> Seq.iter(fun c -> c.Send results)

        server.Start(fun socket ->
                        socket.OnOpen <- fun () -> socketOnOpen socket
                        socket.OnClose <- fun () -> socketOnClose socket
                        socket.OnMessage <- fun message ->
                                                socketOnMessage message)

        Console.ReadLine() |> ignore)
```

The two type definitions and the defined agent are exactly the same as what we had in the IIS 8 example. The emphasized code instantiates a `WebSocketServer`; defines three methods to handle socket open events, socket close events, and messaging events, respectively; and starts up the server.

To use it, all you have to do is change the JavaScript `uri` assignment in the previously shown JavaScript code to point at the URL of the Fleck server and clear your browser cache. In the end, the application works exactly as it did in the IIS 8 example.

Using SignalR

I think we all will agree that Web Sockets is pretty cool. The type of bidirectional communication it affords opens up a world of opportunity. Unfortunately, support for Web Sockets is still spotty. So, while Web Sockets is certainly a glimpse of the future, it may not seem like a viable option for the systems you are building today. If only we had some way to take advantage of Web Sockets when it is available, but fall back to other options when it isn't.

As I'm sure you have guessed, this is certainly achievable, and one option for doing so is built into a set of libraries named SignalR. SignalR is something that two Microsoft employees started as an open source project that was later adopted by Microsoft as an officially sponsored project. SignalR makes it easy to build real-time solutions using asynchronous signaling approaches. SignalR makes it possible for us to build modern solutions today that will automatically take advantage of Web Sockets when available.

So what does SignalR do when Web Sockets support isn't available? It checks for a few different options, and uses the one that is best suited to the task at hand. Web Sockets is checked first. If that isn't supported then Server-Sent Events, Forever Frame, and Long Polling are checked.

SignalR isn't the only game in town when it comes to falling back to other techniques such as Forever Frame and Long Polling. Socket.IO and NowJS are a few options that do this as well. However, SignalR goes about it in an easier way and is specifically designed to play well with ASP.NET.

Building a Persistent Connection Example

Two primary options are available for building the SignalR server-side aspects. The first is a persistent connection and the second is a hub. The persistent connection option is pretty similar to what we've seen in the Fleck and IIS 8 web socket server implementations provided in this chapter.

As you'll see, it doesn't take much code to get this set up. You start by installing the SignalR NuGet package. After that, it's a simple matter of adding a custom route map and implementing a class that derives from `PersistentConnection`. A snippet from a *Global.fs* file with the new code emphasized is shown in the following example:

```
type Global() =
    inherit System.Web.HttpApplication()

    static member RegisterRoutes(routes:RouteCollection) =
        routes.IgnoreRoute("{resource}.axd/{*pathInfo}")
        routes.MapRoute("Default",
                        "{controller}/{action}/{id}",
                        { controller = "Home"; action = "Index"
                          id = UrlParameter.Optional } )

    member this.Start() =
        RouteTable.Routes
            .MapConnection<ChartServer>("chartserver",
                                        "chartserver/{*operation}") |> ignore

        AreaRegistration.RegisterAllAreas()
        Global.RegisterRoutes(RouteTable.Routes)
```

The new class that inherits `PersistentConnection` is shown in the next example. As I mentioned, it's not that much different from the previously shown IIS 8 web socket server examples. Here we're simply overriding the `OnReceivedAsync` method rather than the `OnMessage` method:

```
module SignalRExample

open System
open SignalR
open Newtonsoft.Json

// Code from previous examples removed for brevity
```

```
type ChartServer() =
    inherit PersistentConnection()

    override x.OnReceivedAsync(request, connectionId, data) =
        votesAgent.PostAndReply(fun reply -> Message.Vote(data, reply))
        |> Seq.map(fun v -> { language = fst v; count = snd v } )
        |> JsonConvert.SerializeObject
        |> base.Connection.Broadcast
```

A JavaScript Client

The client-side aspects of SignalR change slightly depending on whether the client is using JavaScript or F# as well as whether the server is using `PersistentConnection` or Hub. Additionally, the JavaScript option is a little bit different from the previously seen web socket client-related JavaScript. This difference is partially due to the jQuery plug-in that helps SignalR do its magic. Here is a JavaScript example for the `Persistent Connection` that we built in the earlier example:

```
/* Some code removed for brevity */

var connection = $.connection("/chartserver");

connection.received(function (data) {
    updateChart($.parseJSON(data));
});

$('#vote').click(function (event) {
    var vote = $('input:radio[name=langOption]:checked');

    if (vote.length) {
        connection.send(vote.val());
    };

    $pages.hide();
    $("#results").toggle();

    event.preventDefault();
});

connection.start();
```

Using the client and server together results in the same effect we achieved in the previous web socket examples. The output looks just like Figure 4-2.

An F# Client

What if you want to connect to a SignalR server from F# instead of JavaScript? That's no problem at all. The next example shows an F# console application that can cast a vote for a favorite programming language.

To build this, create a new F# console application, install the `SignalR.Client` NuGet package, and add code such as the following:

```
module SignalRExample

open System
open SignalR.Client

let connection =
    Connection "http://localhost:2920/chartserver"

connection.Start().Wait()

connection.Send "F#"
|> Async.AwaitIAsyncResult
|> Async.Ignore
|> ignore

connection.Stop() |> ignore

printfn "Vote cast for F#"
Console.ReadLine() |> ignore
```

Constructing a Hub Example

As I mentioned previously, SignalR provides another option, which is known as a `Hub`. This option provides a higher-level abstraction over `PersistentConnection`. This abstraction makes it possible for the server to call named JavaScript functions. Let's look at an example.

The server side

The next example provides a self-hosted SignalR Hub. It's an F# console application that has had the `SignalR.Hosting.Self` package installed. To set up the hub, you create a class that inherits from `Hub`. You then add the methods you wish to be available for calls from clients. To call functions declared in JavaScript, you can use the `Clients` dynamic object followed by the name of the desired function. This code is emphasized in the following example:

```
// Code from previous examples removed for brevity

type ChartHub() =
    inherit Hub()
    member x.Send (data:string) =
        let result =
            votesAgent.PostAndReply(fun reply -> Message.Vote(data, reply))
            |> Seq.map(fun v -> { language = fst v; count = snd v } )
        try
            base.Clients?updateChart(result)
        with
```

```
    | ex ->
        printfn "%s" ex.Message

let server = Server "http://*:8181/"
server.MapHubs() |> ignore

server.Start()

printfn "Now listening on port 8181"
Console.ReadLine() |> ignore
```

One thing you may have noticed in the preceding example is the use of the ? operator when working with the dynamic Clients object. F# doesn't provide the exact same dynamic object option that is provided in C#. Instead, it provides a more powerful option that allows you to implement whatever dynamic functionality you require. This option is provided in the form of *dynamic lookup operators*.

Dynamic lookup operators can provide the same functionality as what is offered in C#, though they're not restricted to that functionality only. You can customize the implementation of dynamic lookup operators in whatever way you see fit, allowing power beyond that of its cousin language. One implementation that has gained popularity is available via the ImpromptuInterface.FSharp library, which can be installed with a NuGet package ID of the same name. The Hub example uses this library.

The client side

The JavaScript code changes slightly when using a Hub as well. Here's the example we have been reviewing, with the changes that are required to interact with a Hub emphasized:

```
$.connection.hub.url = 'http://localhost:8181/signalr'

var chartHub = $.connection.chartHub;

chartHub.updateChart = function (data) {
    updateChart(data);
};

$('#vote').click(function (event) {
    var vote = $('input:radio[name=langOption]:checked');

    if (vote.length) {
        chartHub.send(vote.val())
    }

    $pages.hide();
    $("#results").toggle();
```

```
      event.preventDefault();
});

$.connection.hub.start();
```

One other key thing we have to do to make this work is to add a few script references such as the following:

```
<script src="@Url.Content("~/Scripts/jquery.signalR-0.5.2.min.js")"></script>
<script src="http://localhost:8181/signalr/hubs" type="text/javascript"></script>
```

Going Mobile

Adding support for mobile devices that also interact with SignalR is pretty easy now that we have the basics built. In this section I'll show a few different approaches for extending the simple survey application to mobile devices. The first uses jQuery Mobile. The second is a native Windows Phone 7 application.

The jQuery Mobile Approach

I've shown several examples throughout this book that use jQuery Mobile and I mentioned briefly how you can quickly configure ASP.NET MVC 4 to react differently for different devices. However, I haven't actually shown an example of this in action. Since we already have a web version of the survey application in place, this is a perfect opportunity to quickly walk through what is needed to switch out the views in an ASP.NET MVC 4 web application when a page is accessed by a mobile device.

You first need to add a new _Layout.cshtml file named _Layout.mobile.cshtml. The typical jQuery Mobile references are then added to this new _Layout file along with the same SignalR, D3, and mainModule JavaScript references that were included in the original _Layout file.

All we need to do now is to make a few adjustments to the HTML in the existing Index.cshtml file. With these changes, the one Index.cshtml file can be reused for both views. The markup, with changes emphasized, is as follows:

```
<div id="survey" class="page" data-role="page" >
  <div class="row" data-role="content">
    <form class="well">
      <fieldset data-role="controlgroup">
        <legend>What is your favorite programming language?</legend>
        <div class="controls">
          <label class="radio">
            <input type="radio" name="langOption" id="fsharp" value="F#" />F#
          </label>
          <label class="radio">
            <input type="radio" name="langOption" id="csharp" value="C#" />C#
          </label>
          <label class="radio">
```

```
            <input type="radio" name="langOption" id="erlang" value="Erlang" />
            Erlang
          </label>
          <label class="radio">
            <input type="radio" name="langOption" id="javascript"
              value="JavaScript" />
            JavaScript
          </label>
          <label class="radio">
            <input type="radio" name="langOption" id="other" value="Other" />
            Other
          </label>
        </div>
      </fieldset>
      <div class="buttonContainer"><button id="vote" class="btn" />
        Cast Vote</div>
    </form>
  </div>
</div>

<div id="results" class="page" data-role="page" >
  <div id="barChart" class="barChart" data-role="content" >
  </div>
</div>
```

 Instead of using the same *Index.cshtml* for both views, we could have created a new ASP.NET MVC view named *Index.mobile.cshtml* to house mobile-specific markup. This is a workable approach if we need to have completely different markup for specific device types; however, I believe it is best to try to keep the markup the same for both views and use media types and other adaptive and/or responsive design techniques to tailor the experience appropriately.

We can verify that things are working by switching out the user agent (*http://googlesys tem.blogspot.com/2011/12/changing-user-agent-new-google-chrome.html*) in a browser such as Chrome. Additionally, we can use emulators and/or simulators such as Testi-Phone (*http://www.testiphone.com/*) to see how things will look when displayed on screens of different sizes. The new look with an iPhone 5 user agent on a simulator is shown in Figure 4-3.

Adding Windows Phone

While the jQuery Mobile approach will work for all the major mobile players, we may wish to develop specific native apps that also take advantage of SignalR. As an example, perhaps we wish to take our simple survey application and create a native Windows Phone 7 version. The resultant visual aspects of the app are shown in Figure 4-4.

Figure 4-3. jQuery Mobile survey

Figure 4-4. Windows Phone 7 survey

A deep dive into how to create Windows Phone 7 applications in F# could easily fill another book. However, you don't need to read a whole other book to quickly get a simple Windows Phone 7 app with F# up and running. Simply install the Windows Phone SDK (*http://www.microsoft.com/en-us/download/details.aspx?id=27570*), then install one of the F# and C# Windows Phone project templates from Visual Studio Gallery, such as the one here (*http://bit.ly/TM5gTd*).

I won't spend a lot of time going into the details of the non-SignalR aspects of this example. You can find the full source at the GitHub website (*http://bit.ly/XdMPgr*). One other thing to point out is that this example uses a self-hosted, persistent connection SignalR server. The code for this is available here (*http://bit.ly/RWNUob*).

At the time of this writing, the Windows Phone 7 development tools are not yet supported in Visual Studio 2012. Because of this, the example provided in this section uses Visual Studio 2010.

After creating a new F# Windows Phone 7 project, we can add the desired XAML (*http://bit.ly/fs-web-cloud*) to make things appear as shown in Figure 4-4. Next, we need to install the `SignalR.Client` NuGet package in both the App and AppHost projects. We're now ready to modify the *AppLogic.fs* file so that it interacts with the SignalR server.

To get started, we'll first create a record that will act as a `Model` as well as a class to act as a `ViewModel`. To keep things simple, I've hardcoded the language choices and associated box color. Each of these is shown in the following example:

```
type LanguageChoice = { Language : string; BoxColor : string }

type LanguageChoiceViewModel() =
    member x.LanguageChoices =
        let result = List<LanguageChoice>()
        result.Add { Language = "F#"; BoxColor = "#F29925" }
        result.Add { Language = "C#"; BoxColor = "#5492CD" }
        result.Add { Language = "Erlang"; BoxColor = "#E41F26" }
        result.Add { Language = "JavaScript"; BoxColor = "#70BE46" }
        result.Add { Language = "Other"; BoxColor = "#535353" }
        result
```

Model-View-ViewModel (MVVM) is a common design pattern that is often used when building XAML-based solutions. You can find more information about MVVM on John Gossman's blog (*http://blogs.msdn.com/b/johngossman/archive/2005/10/08/478683.aspx*). It should be noted that the example provided in this section does not follow MVVM fully. Instead, the example is optimized for simplicity and set up to show different approaches.

Now that the Model and ViewModel are created, we can modify the MainPage class to include the logic needed to send the selected vote information to the SignalR server. The code to accomplish this is shown in the next example and I'll point out various interesting aspects in the next several paragraphs:

```
type MainPage() as this =
    inherit PhoneApplicationPage()
    do this.DataContext <- LanguageChoiceViewModel()
    do Application.LoadComponent(this,
        new System.Uri("/WindowsPhoneApp;component/MainPage.xaml",
            System.UriKind.Relative))

    let confirmationLabel : TextBlock = this?Confirmation

    member this.AnswerButton_Click(sender:obj, e:RoutedEventArgs) =
        let answerButton = sender :?> Button
        SignalR.connection.Send(answerButton.Tag)
            .Start(TaskScheduler.FromCurrentSynchronizationContext())
        confirmationLabel.Text <- "Thanks for Voting!"
```

The first few lines of code in this class are wiring up the class to the XAML. The class inherits PhoneApplicationPage, sets our ViewModel as the DataContext, and finally associates *MainPage.xaml* to the class.

The next line locates the TextBlock with a name of Confirmation in the XAML and binds it to a value named confirmationLabel. This shows a little bit of the power of the dynamic lookup operator that I talked about previously in this chapter. In the default output of this Windows Phone 7 project template, an implementation of the dynamic lookup operator is provided with the primary goal of locating resources in a Resource Dictionary or finding controls in XAML.

The AnswerButton_Click member shows a traditional code-behind type of click event handler. This is where we see the first mention of anything related to SignalR. Within this event handler, we determine which button was pressed and send the information to the SignalR server by starting the task from the current synchronization context. Lastly, the text of a label is set to a desired confirmation message.

The only other thing to discuss is how the SignalR server connection information is determined. In this example, this is accomplished by defining a module with a function named startConnection. This function is called whenever the application launches. Conversely, the connection is stopped whenever the application is closed. Here is the code for defining the module with the startConnection function:

```
module SignalR =
    let connection =
        Connection "http://localhost:8081/chartserver"
```

```
let startConnection() =
    if connection.State = ConnectionState.Disconnected then
        connection.Start().Start(
            TaskScheduler.FromCurrentSynchronizationContext())
```

Combining F# and NoSQL

NoSQL data storage options have been gaining in popularity over the past few years. This class of data store breaks away from the traditional RDBMS databases that have ruled for so long. NoSQL databases generally store data in unstructured or semi-structured formats rather than with the strict schemas used in relational databases. This approach makes it easier to scale horizontally, support redundancy, and handle massive amounts of data while making insertion and retrieval of that data amazingly fast. If you want to achieve faster and more scalable F# solutions that work well for both mobile and web applications, you'll definitely want to learn about NoSQL databases and how to interact with them through F#.

In this section, I'll show you how to use F# to interact with a few document-oriented NoSQL options. I'll use a simple example of a basic grid that lists a minimal amount of information (first name, last name, and phone number) for a contact list. Additionally, a simple form for creating new contacts is provided. Since the primary focus is to show methods for getting started with inserting and retrieving records from these databases, I won't spend much time on the UI aspects. You can see the full examples here (*https:// github.com/dmohl/fs-web-cloud-mobile/tree/master/Ch%204*).

MongoDB

MongoDB is one of the most popular NoSQL options in the .NET space. Like the other NoSQL databases discussed in this section, MongoDB is a document-oriented database. This means information pushed in the database is stored with a key and an associated document. When a document is later requested by the key, retrieval is exceptionally fast. Instructions on setting up MongoDB on Windows are available here (*http://bit.ly/ mongodb-windows*).

Once you follow the steps for getting MongoDB up and running, the next step is to create a client to interact with that instance. The easiest way to get up and running with Mon-goDB and F# is to install the NuGet package with ID MongoFs into a project. This will pull the official C# MongoDB client as well as a simple F# wrapper that helps make interaction with the C# MongoDB client API from F# a little nicer.

As I mentioned previously, I will be showing a simple example for each of the three document-oriented data stores discussed in this section. Each example is an ASP.NET MVC 4 project that was set up with the C#/F# ASP.NET MVC 4 template that we discussed in Chapter 1. The example uses a record called Contact, as shown here:

```
namespace FsWeb.Models

open MongoDB.Bson
open System.ComponentModel.DataAnnotations

[<CLIMutable>]
type Contact = {
    _id : ObjectId
    [<Required>] FirstName : string
    [<Required>] LastName : string
    [<Required>] Phone : string
}
```

There are two aspects of this code that probably need a little explanation. The first is the `ObjectId` type. `ObjectId` is a 12-byte binary type provided by MongoDB. This type is commonly used as the unique ID for documents.

The second aspect is the `CLIMutable` attribute, which I briefly mentioned in all of the chapters up to this point. This attribute is a lesser-known feature of F# 3.0 that has tremendous value when working with records that need to be serialized or deserialized, such as when going to or from a document data store. When the F# compiler sees the attribute it automatically adds a parameterless constructor as well as getters and setters for the properties. This one little attribute opens the door for records to be used in places that were previously more difficult, such as in the controllers of an ASP.NET MVC application.

The code needed to retrieve all the stored contacts from MongoDB, as well as create new contacts, is shown in the following example:

```
namespace FsWeb.Controllers

open System.Linq
open System.Web
open System.Web.Mvc
open FsWeb.Models

[<HandleError>]
type HomeController() =
    inherit Controller()

    let contacts =
        createLocalMongoServer()
        |> getMongoDatabase "contactDb"
        |> getMongoCollection "contacts"

    member this.Index () =
        contacts.FindAll().ToList() |> this.View

    [<HttpGet>]
    member this.Create () =
        this.View()
```

```
[<HttpPost>]
member this.Create (contact:Contact) =
    if base.ModelState.IsValid then
        contact |> contacts.Insert |> ignore
        this.RedirectToAction("Index") :> ActionResult
    else
        this.View() :> ActionResult
```

The emphasized code shows how little is needed to interact with MongoDB from F# when using MongoFs. The first four emphasized lines identify the MongoDB instance, database, and collection with which you wish to interact. Additionally, if the database or collection doesn't already exist, it will be created. The pipelining approach used to accomplish these tasks is provided by the MongoFs library. The one line required for retrieving all records as well as the one line needed to insert a contact are achieved solely by the great syntax of F# combined with the API of the official C# MongoDB client.

One other thing you may have noticed is that I never open the MongoFs module in this example. This is due to another feature of F#, called the AutoOpen attribute. When the AutoOpen attribute is added to a module, that module will not need to be explicitly opened or referenced. Here's an example of the AutoOpen attribute in use:

```
[<AutoOpen>]
Module MongoFs

// Code removed for brevity
```

RavenDB

RavenDB is another document-oriented database that has been taking the world by storm. A few of the big benefits of RavenDB include support for transactions, full-text search via Lucene, a "safe by default" core principle, and ease of embedding the DB when desired.

For the example that follows, download and extract the latest build of RavenDB (*http://builds.hibernatingrhinos.com/builds/RavenDB*). You can then launch the RavenDB server. Once that is complete, you should be able to run the example (*https://github.com/dmohl/fs-web-cloud-mobile/tree/master/Ch%204/RavenExample*). The example was built by installing version 1.0.960 of the RavenDB.Client.FSharp NuGet package into an F#/C# ASP.NET MVC solution. The code needed to get our contacts list up and running is shown in the following example:

```
namespace FsWeb.Controllers

open System.Linq
open System.Web
open System.Web.Mvc
open FsWeb.Models
open Raven.Client.Document
```

```
[<HandleError>]
type HomeController() =
    inherit Controller()

    let ravenUrl = "http://localhost:8080/"

    let executeRavenAction action =
        use store = new DocumentStore()
        store.Url <- ravenUrl
        store.Initialize() |> ignore
        use session = store.OpenSession()
        action session

    member this.Index () =
        executeRavenAction
        <| fun session -> session.Query<Contact>().ToList()
        |> this.View

    [<HttpGet>]
    member this.Create () =
        this.View()

    [<HttpPost>]
    member this.Create (contact:Contact) =
        if base.ModelState.IsValid then
            executeRavenAction
            <| fun session ->
                session.Store contact
                session.SaveChanges()
            this.RedirectToAction("Index") :> ActionResult
        else
            this.View() :> ActionResult
```

While the code is a bit more verbose than the MongoDB example, you get a few key
benefits such as inherent usage of the Unit of Work pattern. In addition to showing the
RavenDB F# client (*http://nuget.org/packages/RavenDB.Client.FSharp/1.0.972*) API in
use, the preceding code also showcases a higher-order function named executeRave
nAction that abstracts away the common code that is used for the majority of interac-
tions with RavenDB.

CouchDB

The last NoSQL option that I will showcase is CouchDB. Built with Erlang, CouchDB
is one of the most fault-tolerant NoSQL options available. It's also easy to distribute and
fast. You can find out more about CouchDB here (*http://couchdb.apache.org/*).

The creator of CouchDB is now primarily focusing on a project called Couchbase, which has a different API and a number of additional features. I have chosen to only show CouchDB in this book; however, I recommend checking out Couchbase to see if it is right for you. A comparison of CouchDB and Couchbase is available here (*http:// vschart.com/compare/couchdb/vs/couchbase*).

There are a number of client options for interacting with CouchDB. One of these options is one that I created, called FSharpCouch. To use it, install the `FSharpCouch` NuGet package in the desired project and use any of the functions described here (*https:// github.com/dmohl/FSharpCouch*). Here's a quick example using the same contacts list application that was shown in the examples for the other two NoSQL options:

```
namespace FsWeb.Controllers

open System.Linq
open System.Web
open System.Web.Mvc
open FsWeb.Models
open FSharpCouch

[<HandleError>]
type HomeController() =
    inherit Controller()

    let couchUrl = "http://localhost:5984"
    let dbName = "people"

    member this.Index () =
        getAllDocuments<Contact> couchUrl dbName
        |> Seq.map(fun c -> c.body)
        |> this.View

    [<HttpGet>]
    member this.Create () =
        this.View()

    [<HttpPost>]
    member this.Create (contact:Contact) =
        if base.ModelState.IsValid then
            contact |> createDocument couchUrl dbName |> ignore
            this.RedirectToAction("Index") :> ActionResult
        else
            this.View() :> ActionResult
```

One interesting aspect of this implementation is that F# records are used without any mutation required. The `Contact` record used for the create request only includes the things directly related, such as first name, last name, and phone. However, the entity or entities that are returned from a create or from either of the get options will return a record that includes an ID and a revision. This is made possible by returning the record shown in the following, with body set to a populated instance of a record that matches what was originally added (this is the main reason for the Seq.map call in the Index method of the previous example):

```
type CouchDocument<'a> = {
    id : string
    rev : string
    body : 'a
}
```

Summary

This chapter covered a few additional approaches that can help you build faster and more scalable web and mobile solutions with F# and other technologies. You learned a few different ways to create and consume Web Sockets as well as various options for interacting with a few common document-oriented data stores. Throughout the chapter, I introduced and explained a handful of features of F# of which you may not have previously been aware.

In the next chapter, I'll show you a few options for creating frontend code with the beauty and elegance of a functional style. The options discussed in the next chapter will allow you to build full stacks using functional concepts and will open your eyes to new thoughts and ideas. You won't want to miss it!

CHAPTER 5

Functional Frontend Development

*The art challenges the technology, and the
technology inspires the art.*

—John Lasseter

For as long as I can remember, I've been playing the guitar. I grew up traveling around on weekends playing in my parents' musical group. This instilled within me a love for the combination of "science" (i.e., music theory, etc.) and art.

 You can hear some of my original music here (*http://www.daniel mohl.com*).

When I first started working with programming languages, the experience brought out similar feelings. While computer programming has many aspects that fit into the science category, the creation of simple, elegant, and beautiful code is certainly an art.

Throughout this book, I've shown you a variety of ways to use F# to create web, mobile, and cloud solutions. Throughout this journey, the F# aspects of the solutions were generally focused on the server side. The examples have increasingly added more and more functional concepts into the mix and the implementation of these concepts has made the solutions more elegant and beautiful. It would be nice to take these concepts and make them available for development of frontend code.

As we all know, JavaScript is the primary language for client-side web development. I really like JavaScript, especially the functional aspects of it. However, it would be great if there were even more functional features. Is there any way that we can make JavaScript even more functional than it already is? The answer, of course, is yes, and there are a number of libraries (*http://ibm.co/U2iuO3*), articles (*http://bit.ly/ben-alman*), and books (*http://bit.ly/udon-javascript*) that talk about implementing common functional concepts in JavaScript.

One of the recent trends in the web world is the use of various tools to compile a variety of programming languages down to JavaScript. The use of these tools makes it possible to more easily add additional functional features to the syntax you use to create the JavaScript code for your solutions.

In this chapter, I will deviate slightly from the focus of the previous chapters. I will point out a few options available to you for creating web-centric, client-side code with a functional style, not all of which are 100% F#. Since the JavaScript approach has been covered by others, I will only focus on the compiler options.

Setting the Stage

Throughout this chapter, we will follow a common template. I'll start by introducing the language and/or tool the section is covering. I'll then talk about some of the benefits of that particular tool, move into information regarding how to get started with it, and finally provide an example of using it to create an application.

Each of the three options presented in this chapter has a number of advantages. As such, the one that is considered to be the "best" will depend on the problem you are trying to solve, the team that is trying to solve it, the development and/or architectural goals of the solution, and personal preference.

The example we will use to show the differences between each option is a simple "To Do" list tracker. It's far from full-featured, but it provides an adequate playground to show off various aspects of the tools in question. The main page of the application provides two groupings of tasks, which clearly separate those that are yet to be done from those that are completed. Once complete, a task can be dragged from the To Do column and dropped into the Done column. Figure 5-1 shows a screenshot of the app.

In addition to the JavaScript generated by the respective compiler, the examples all use jQuery and jQuery UI. The examples also use CSS from jQuery UI and Twitter Bootstrap. Let's get on with the show!

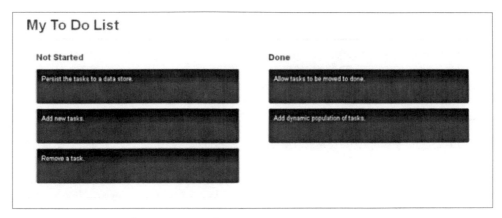

Figure 5-1. To Do application screenshot

Looking at LiveScript

If you have been in the web space for long, the first thought that went through your head when you saw the word *LiveScript* may have been that this was the original name for JavaScript. While the name previously referenced the well-known client-scripting language, it is currently being rebranded to refer to a language that compiles to JavaScript.

The main LiveScript website (*http://gkz.github.com/LiveScript/*) states that the language "is a fork of Coco, which is in turn derived from CoffeeScript." It has inherited all the good things from these other languages and added new features and functionality that better facilitate development using a functional style.

Benefits

LiveScript offers a number of benefits, but I'm going to focus on the ones that have some relation to F#. While LiveScript doesn't use the exact same syntax as F#, as do the other options mentioned in this chapter, it does include a number of concepts and features that directly relate to similar concepts and features in F#.

 This is not intended to be a comprehensive list of all the features of LiveScript. For a full list and a wide variety of examples, visit the LiveScript website (*http://gkz.github.com/LiveScript/*) and read this (*http://bit.ly/programming-javascript*) and this (*http://bit.ly/javascript-part2*).

The first feature that relates very well to the F# language is the use of significant whitespace. As with F#, LiveScript uses spaces to delineate blocks of code. Additionally, parentheses, commas, braces, and brackets are often optional. This makes your code concise, yet readable.

As I previously mentioned, LiveScript includes a variety of functional features that correspond well with similar features in F#. Some of these include curried functions and partial application, basic pattern matching, a pipe-forward operator and pipe-backward operator using |> and <|, and function composition using >> and <<. Using prelude.ls —which is a library written by the same author as LiveScript—with LiveScript adds a variety of higher-order functions such as map, filter, head, tail, fold, cons, append, zip, and much more.

Since LiveScript originated from CoffeeScript, which has a motto of "It's Just JavaScript," your current JavaScript skills give you a nice head start on writing LiveScript. Additionally, the JavaScript that the compiler generates is very readable. These two aspects of the language make it fairly easy to debug and allow for seamless integration with any other JavaScript libraries.

Usage

The recommended way to get up and running with LiveScript is to use the Node Package Manager to install the LiveScript package (i.e., npm install -g LiveScript) or to clone the GitHub repo and install LiveScript from the clone. This of course means that Node.js must be installed on your machine. If you haven't used Node, never fear. It's super easy to get set up. Visit the Node.js website (*http://nodejs.org/*) for information.

 If you just want to play with LiveScript and don't want to go through the trouble of setting everything up, you can simply go to the LiveScript website on GitHub (*http://gkz.github.com/LiveScript/*), which includes an online REPL.

Once LiveScript is installed, you can create your first file to compile. These files have a *.ls* extension and whatever you place before this extension will determine the name of the output JavaScript file. For this example, we'll name the file *test.js.ls*. Within this file, add code such as the following:

```
weekend = <[ sat sun ]>

isWeekend = (dayOfWeek) ->
    | dayOfWeek in weekend => true
    | _ => false

'sun' |> isWeekend |> console.log
```

Much of this code should look pretty familiar to you as the syntax is fairly close to various F# code we have already gone over. The first line in this example is creating an array of strings. The next three lines of code define a function named isWeekend that takes one argument. Basic pattern matching is then done to determine whether the provided string is contained in the weekend array. Lastly, we use the pipe-forward operator to determine whether the string sun is part of the weekend, the result of which is then piped to console.log.

To compile this code down to JavaScript, run the following command from the command line (where *src/* is the directory that contains the *.ls* files and *lib/* is the desired output directory):

```
livescript --compile --output lib/ src/
```

You can then use the JavaScript file that is generated from this command in the same way you would normally use any other JavaScript file.

Example

Now that I've shown you a very simple example, it's time to put this knowledge to use to build a slightly more complicated, slightly more real-world example. This is the first working example of our "To Do" drag-and-drop application that I mentioned previously in this chapter. Since I already showed you what the screen will look like once we're done, let's dive right into the code.

To provide a little more context, here's the markup we will be working with:

```
<div role="main">
    <div class="container todoList">
        <h1>My To Do List</h1>
        <div class="detail row-fluid">
            <div class="span6 taskContainer well">
                <div class="column-header">
                    <h3>Not Started</h3>
                </div>
                <div class="tasks tasksNotStarted droppable">
                </div>
            </div>
            <div class="span6 taskContainer well">
                <div class="column-header">
                    <h3>Done</h3>
                </div>
                <div class="tasks tasksDone droppable"/>
            </div>
        </div>
    </div>
</div>
```

The LiveScript code used to make everything work is as follows:

```
let $ = jQuery
    # Adds each task to the appropriate DIV
    populateTaskList = ( $el, taskList ) ->
        taskList
```

```
            |> prelude.each ( (t) ->
                $ "<div class='ui-widget-content draggable'>#{t}</div>"
                .appendTo $el )

        # Initializer
        do ->
            tasksToDo = [ "Persist the tasks to a data store."
                "Add new tasks."
                "Remove a task." ]
            tasksDone = [ "Allow tasks to be moved to done."
                "Add dynamic population of tasks." ]

            populateTaskList $( ".tasksNotStarted" ), tasksToDo
            populateTaskList $( ".tasksDone" ), tasksDone

        # Define the draggable elements.
        $ ".draggable" .draggable (
            revert: "invalid"
            cursor: "move"
            helper: "clone"
        )

        # Setup the droppable areas
        $ ".droppable" .droppable (
            hoverClass: "ui-state-active"
            accept: ".draggable"
            drop: ( event, ui ) -> ui.draggable.appendTo $ @
        )
```

The # symbol denotes a comment in LiveScript.

Let's walk through this code piece by piece. The first line causes the rest of the code to be wrapped in a self-executing anonymous function. Additionally, it ensures that $ is set to jQuery, just in case something else has changed the meaning of $. Both of these are considered to be good practices in the JavaScript world.

Next, a function named populateTaskList is defined. This function takes two parameters. The first represents the element to which the specific tasks are being added and the second is an array of text that represents different tasks. The array of tasks is then piped into a function provided by prelude.ls named each, which causes a div to be created for each task and added to the specified container element.

I could have simply used the `jQuery.each` function in the example rather than `prelude.each`, thus eliminating one dependency. However, `prelude.ls` includes a number of very useful functions that are not currently part of jQuery, so I chose to leave this as a simple example of how to use `prelude.ls`.

The next piece of code creates a self-executing anonymous function that simply defines two arrays and then passes them on to another function for processing. The first array contains the text for each task that is yet to be done and the second contains the text for tasks that are complete. Each array is then passed to the `populateTaskList` function along with the specific element to which each task in the provided list should be added.

The last two main aspects of this example specify which elements are draggable and which are droppable. This uses the standard jQuery UI API. There are a couple of things worth pointing out here. First, you'll notice that various characters such as parentheses, commas, and semicolons are missing. We can thank Coco for the ability to leave out the parens (e.g., `$ ".draggable"`), which as I said before is one of the parents of LiveScript. The ability to skip adding commas and semicolons is inherited from features provided by CoffeeScript. These are specific examples of some of the optional characters I mentioned previously. The second thing to point out is the use of `@` in the definition of the function that is triggered when a drop event occurs. `@` is simply a shorter way to write the `this` JavaScript keyword.

LiveScript provides a nice way to stay fairly close to JavaScript, while still being able to use more of a functional style. It seamlessly integrates with any other JavaScript libraries and, though young, is quite stable due to its heritage. The full source for this example is available here (*http://bit.ly/livescript*).

Exploring Pit

While LiveScript provides a nice way to write our web-centric client code in a functional style, it still isn't F#. It would be great if we could actually use real F# code to create that client-side JavaScript. This is where Pit comes in.

Pit was created by Fahad Suhaib and Karthik Vishnu and is built from the ground up in F#. It was first checked into GitHub in December 2011 and since it isn't a fork of some predecessor, it's the youngest of the options that I discuss in this chapter.

Let's explore some of the benefits that Pit provides.

Benefits

Pit provides a couple of different options for initiating compilation. The first option is to compile code by executing the Pit compiler with specific parameters via the command line (similar to how we compiled LiveScript). The second is to leverage the Visual Studio or MonoDevelop integration to create a project and allow that project to take care of passing the correct commands to the compiler. If you're already using Visual Studio and/or MonoDevelop, this second option can make it very easy to get up and running. This also means there are no external dependencies such as Node.js.

The biggest benefit that Pit provides over something like LiveScript is that it's all F#. This is great because you can take most of what you've already learned about F# and apply it immediately to creating web-centric, client-side code. A full listing of the F# features that are supported in Pit is available here (*http://bit.ly/pitfw-docs*).

The last benefit I will point out is the debug story that Pit provides. Pit supports two modes of compilation: debug and release. When compiled in debug mode, Pit uses the Silverlight runtime along with a Silverlight-to-JavaScript bridge to provide an elegant debugging story. Since most of the available offerings that compile higher-level languages down to JavaScript lack in the area of debugging support, this can be a big benefit. To learn more about this feature, read the document mentioned in the preceding paragraph.

 A new feature called source maps promises to solve the debugging support problems of the various tools that compile to JavaScript. You can see an example here (*http://www.youtube.com/watch?v=-xJl22Kvgjg*).

Usage

The quickest way to get started with Pit on Windows is to download the build (*http://pitfw.org/*), extract the *Pit.Setup.msi* file, and then launch it to install Pit. This will add the Pit compiler executable (*pfc.exe*) and the supporting libraries to a directory named *Pit* in the 32-bit version of the *program files* directory. Additionally, a Visual Studio extension is executed during the process, which adds a few new project templates to help you quickly get up and running with Pit in Visual Studio 2010.

You may have noticed that the preceding paragraph mentions running Pit in Visual Studio 2010. At the time of this writing, Pit currently only supports Visual Studio 2010, though support for Visual Studio 2012 is on the road map along with a number of other great new features. There are a few ways to use Pit with a Visual Studio 2012 solution today. The first is to simply use it from the command line. A second option is to manually tweak the Visual Studio extension (VSIX) package used to add the project templates so that it recognizes Visual Studio 2012. You can quickly do this by renaming the VSIX to have a *.zip* extension, cracking it open, modifying the `SupportedProducts` element in the *extension.vsixmanifest* so that it looks like the following example, and finally compressing all the files into a file with a *.vsix* extension; you can then execute the VSIX to have the templates installed into Visual Studio 2012:

```
<SupportedProducts>
  <VisualStudio Version="11.0">
    <Edition>Ultimate</Edition>
    <Edition>Premium</Edition>
    <Edition>Pro</Edition>
  </VisualStudio>
  <VisualStudio Version="10.0">
    <Edition>Ultimate</Edition>
    <Edition>Premium</Edition>
    <Edition>Pro</Edition>
  </VisualStudio>
</SupportedProducts>
```

 To learn more about creating Visual Studio extensions with F#, see the MSDN article (*http://bit.ly/vsix-template*) on the topic.

I had to do one more thing in order to build the example that appears in the next section. As I said, Pit is actively being improved. Some of the recent improvements include support for jQuery and jQuery UI. In order to take advantage of these improvements, you will need to download the latest stable assemblies (version 0.3.3 at the time of this writing) from the download page on the Pit GitHub site (*http://bit.ly/pitfw-download*).

Once downloaded, you can extract the files and use them to overlay the existing Pit libraries, executable, and JavaScript files (which you can find in a folder such as *C:\Program Files (x86)\Pit\0.2\bin*). Now that we have these basic setup tasks out of the way, we can look at how to build our To Do application.

 Make sure you do not remove the existing files from the *C:\Program Files (x86)\Pit\0.2\bin* directory before copying in the new files.

Example

To build our To Do application, we start by creating an ASP.NET MVC 4 project template. Next, we add the *Pit.Core.js* and *Pit.js* files from the *bin* directory of the Pit installation path and reference them the same way we would any other JavaScript file. We can now add a new Pit Library project, which can be found under Visual F#→Pit in the Project Creation Wizard.

 While this example uses ASP.NET MVC, there's nothing in it currently that would require this. We could have just as easily created only the Pit Library project and used plain old HTML, CSS, and so on, for the rest.

There are a couple of things left to do. First, we'll set up a post build event to automatically copy the generated JavaScript file from the Pit Library project output directory to the *Scripts* directory in the web project. The post build event for the example I built is shown here:

```
copy /Y "$(TargetDir)$(ProjectName).js"
    "$(SolutionDir)PitTodoExample\PitTodoExampleWeb\Scripts\$(ProjectName).js"
```

To use Pit to create the JavaScript needed to make our application work, we need only add one *.fs* file to the Pit Library project. The code that should be placed into this file is as follows:

```
namespace PitTodo

open Pit
open Pit.Dom
open Pit.JavaScript
open Pit.JavaScript.JQuery
open Pit.JavaScript.JQuery.UI

module mainModule =
    [<JsObject>]
    type dragType = { draggable : DomElement }

    [<Js>]
    let populateTaskList (el:DomElement) tasksList =
        tasksList
        |> List.iter( fun (task:string) ->
            tag "div" [|
                "class"@="ui-widget-content draggable"
                "innerHtml"@=task |]
            |> Html.make
            |> el.AppendChild )

    [<Js>]
    let populateTasks () =
        let tasksToDo =
            [ "Persist the tasks to a data store."
              "Add new tasks."
              "Remove a task." ]
        let tasksDone =
            [ "Allow tasks to be moved to done."
              "Add dynamic population of tasks." ]
        let tasksNotStartedEl = document.QuerySelector ".tasksNotStarted"
        let tasksDoneEl = document.QuerySelector ".tasksDone"
        populateTaskList tasksNotStartedEl tasksToDo
        populateTaskList tasksDoneEl tasksDone

    [<Js>]
    let initDragAndDrop () =
        jQueryUI(".draggable")
            .draggable(
```

```
                 [ "revert" => "invalid"
                   "cursor" => "move"
                   "helper" => "clone" ] )
           .ignore()

     jQueryUI(".droppable")
         .droppable(
             [ "hoverClass" => "ui-state-active"
               "accept" => ".draggable"
               "drop" => fun (event, ui:dragType) ->
                   jQuery("this").append(ui.draggable).ignore() ] )
         .ignore()

[<DomEntryPoint>]
[<Js>]
let main() =
    populateTasks()
    initDragAndDrop()
```

The first thing you may notice is the use of various attributes on specific functions and/ or types. This application uses three of the more common attributes. The `JsObject` attribute is used to tell the compiler that a specific record type should be compiled to a JavaScript literal. The `Js` attribute is used to indicate that an F# function, constructor, or member should be compiled to JavaScript. The `DomEntryPoint` attribute specifies the starting point for the application.

 Attributes in Pit such as `Js` are just special cases or aliases for the standard `ReflectedDefinitionAttribute` in F# that returns the code as an abstract syntax tree rather than compiled IL.

The code itself isn't that much different from the LiveScript version, except that you get to use the strongly typed goodness of F# to do it. First, the `dragType` record is defined and decorated so that it will be compiled to a JavaScript object literal. This will be used later when the desired elements are made to be droppable. Next, the `populateTask List` function is used to create `div`s for all the strings in the provided list of strings and each is appended to the specified element. The `populateTasks` function accomplishes the same things as the function with the same name in the LiveScript example. Next, the `initDragAndDrop` function is used to set up the specified elements as draggable or droppable. Finally, the `main` function kicks it all off by calling `populateTasks` followed by `initDragAndDrop`.

If you look at the JavaScript that is generated by Pit, you'll see one big difference between it and that which is generated by LiveScript. While LiveScript primarily uses self-executing anonymous functions to protect the global namespace, Pit uses the namespace pattern. Both work well for accomplishing the desired goal. A good resource for learning about these types of patterns is Stoyan Stefanov's book, *JavaScript Patterns* (O'Reilly).

The full Pit To Do Application example is available here (*http://bit.ly/pittodo*).

Diving into WebSharper

The most well-known F# web application framework is named WebSharper. Of the options that I've presented, WebSharper is the most mature and most proven in production. One of the most well-known sites built with WebSharper is FPish (*http://fpish.net*), which is a full-featured online community for functional programmers. WebSharper is also being used in a number of companies, including Microsoft and Ford.

Like Pit, WebSharper compiles F# to JavaScript. However, it doesn't limit itself to only the generation of JavaScript. Instead, it provides the ability to create all aspects of the full web stack in F#. This means that in addition to client-side and server-side code, you can also create markup in F#. Additionally, WebSharper makes the interaction between the client and server code trivial.

Let's dig into a few more of the benefits.

Benefits

As I previously mentioned, one of the biggest benefits of WebSharper is the ability to create the entire stack in F#. This reduces the context switching that is associated with moving between different syntax, concepts, and idioms. Since the one language is F#, you get the majority of benefits that F# provides, such as type safety, type inference, all of the great out-of-the-box modules such as Seq, and the numerous features of Visual Studio.

WebSharper has done a good job of getting in front of technology trends. The features needed to accommodate these trends are brought into WebSharper and made available for you to use without requiring you to be an expert in any of the particular trending technologies. For example, WebSharper is heavily vested in HTML5, but you won't have to be an expert in HTML5 to use the applicable features. Additionally, WebSharper seamlessly handles the differences between browsers, automatically determines what dependencies are needed by a page and only loads these dependencies, and provides type-safe access to a variety of the most popular libraries via WebSharper extensions. Mobile solutions can be created with ease using extensions for libraries such as jQuery

Mobile, SenchaTouch, and Kendo UI as well as settings that allow these applications to be packaged up as native apps for Android or Windows Phone 7. Yet another example is that Visual Studio 2012 is fully supported and has been since well before the RTM release.

 IntelliFactory CEO Adam Granicz discusses several of the abstractions that WebSharper offers and gives a mobile example in an article he wrote for the InfoQ website (*http://www.infoq.com/articles/WebSharper*).

Ultimately, the goal of WebSharper is to help you create web and mobile solutions more quickly. I've only touched the tip of the iceberg as it relates to the features that Web-Sharper provides to accomplish this goal. I encourage you to check out the WebSharper samples (*http://websharper.com/SamplesPage*).

Usage

Getting started with WebSharper is as easy as installing one or more components, and then using the same Visual Studio project creation features you know and love to create a new project. You can download the core product from the WebSharper Downloads page (*http://websharper.com/downloads*). At the time of writing, WebSharper 2.4 Q2 is the most recent release. Additionally, various extension installers can be downloaded from this page. A variety of WebSharper-related packages can also be found on NuGet.

Once everything is installed, you'll see a new subcategory named WebSharper under Visual F# whenever you start creating a new project. Selecting this subcategory shows a variety of project creation options including solutions for ASP.NET, ASP.NET MVC, Sitelets, and Android. In addition to templates that have only the barebones code needed to start building solutions with WebSharper, there are also templates that provide full examples. These are great options when you are first getting started.

 Sitelets provide a different approach to building MVC applications. The WebSharper website (*http://websharper.com/home*) states that they are a "handy abstraction for composable website components. Sitelets are MVC done right, featuring first-class actions and type-safe cross-links."

For example, the Sample Web Application (Sitelets) project template generates a solution that includes an example of formlets, templating, routing, composition of sitelets, integration with an ASPX page that isn't directly associated with the sitelets, and more. You can learn more about sitelets and formlets here (*http://websharper.com/docs/abstractions*).

There are also a handful of good examples on the Web for building full stacks with WebSharper. Some of these include:

- *http://www.websharper.com/blogs/2011/6/2059*
- *http://www.developerfusion.com/article/124078/building-an-html5-application-with-websharper-sitelets-part-1/*
- *http://v2matveev.blogspot.com/2010/06/playing-with-websharper.html*
- *http://fsharp-code.blogspot.com/2012/07/websharper-slideshow.html*

These, as well as the samples on the WebSharper site (*http://websharper.com*), are also great ways to get started.

Example

A few options are available to us for building the To Do application with WebSharper. While any of them will work, I chose to use the ASP.NET MVC approach since it's the most similar to other concepts already discussed throughout this book. In addition to the solution created by the project template, we'll need to install the WebSharper .JQueryUi NuGet package.

We need a few classes and modules to create this example. However, I'm going to concentrate on the code that generates the task divs and adds the drag-and-drop functionality. The following code provides this functionality:

```
namespace Website

open IntelliFactory.WebSharper
open IntelliFactory.WebSharper.Html
open IntelliFactory.WebSharper.JQuery
open IntelliFactory.WebSharper.JQueryUI

open Website

module Todo =
    [<JavaScript>]
    let initDrag element =
        let config =
            DraggableConfiguration(cursor = "move", helper = "clone")
        Draggable.New(element, config)

    [<JavaScript>]
    let initDrop (element:Html.Element) =
        let config =
            DroppableConfiguration(
                hoverClass = "ui-state-active", accept = ".draggable")
        let dropZone = Droppable.New(element, config)
        dropZone.OnDrop( fun ev el ->
            JQuery.Of(element.Dom).Append(el.Draggable).Ignore )
```

```
        dropZone

    [<JavaScript>]
    let main tasks =
        Div [Attr.Class "droppable"] -< [
            for task in tasks ->
                Div [Attr.Class "ui-widget-content draggable"; Text task]
                |> initDrag ]
        |> initDrop

type IndexControl() =
    inherit Web.Control()

    [<DefaultValue>]
    val mutable Tasks : string list

    [<JavaScript>]
    override x.Body =
        upcast Todo.main x.Tasks
```

As with Pit, an attribute is used to tell the WebSharper compiler that the function should be compiled to JavaScript. The first function in this code that includes this attribute is the initDrag function. This function uses the jQuery UI WebSharper extension to provide strongly typed access to the jQuery UI API. In this case, the function takes an element and makes it draggable.

The initDrop function is similar to the initDrag function in that it uses the jQuery UI WebSharper extension. As the name suggests, this function marks the provided element as being a drop area. It also defines an anonymous function that specifies what should be done when an element is dropped on one of these areas.

The main function is primarily responsible for creating the draggable elements. Additionally, this function handles calling the other functions to provide the appropriate drag-and-drop functionality. This shows a small example of WebSharper's features surrounding strongly typed creation of HTML elements.

Lastly, a type is defined, which inherits from Web.Control. This type calls the main function to kick everything off.

 While this example happens to be for ASP.NET MVC, the type that was defined that inherits from Web.Control could just as easily be embedded in other platforms such as ASP.NET WebForms.

You can find the full example here (*https://github.com/dmohl/fs-web-cloud-mobile/tree/ master/Ch%205/WebSharperTodo*). As I previously mentioned, WebSharper does much, much more than what is shown in this example. The client-side aspects that were showcased within it are just the tip of the iceberg.

Summary

Throughout this book, you've seen how a functional style can make your code simple, succinct, and readable. The tools shown in this chapter allow you to take that style and use it for frontend development. Whether your preference is LiveScript, Pit, WebSharper, or plain old JavaScript, the concepts in this chapter and throughout this book have hopefully opened your mind to new ideas, challenged previous assumptions, and provided inspiration.

It has been a great journey. You've learned how to use F# to build ASP.NET MVC applications, WCF and HTTP services, cloud solutions, mobile solutions, and more. You now have all the tools you need to start building great web, cloud, and mobile solutions with the power of F#. You may be wondering, "Where do I go from here?" The best advice I can give is to go out and use F# to build awesome solutions. The more you use it, the more you will love it!

Useful Tools and Libraries

This appendix takes a look at a few tools and libraries that can enhance your F# web, cloud, and mobile development experience.

FAKE (F# Make)

FAKE is a build tool similar to Make that allows you to automate a sequence of steps that you wish to have done during each build. The permutations of things you might include in the automated build script for a solution are endless, but at a minimum you will likely want to compile all projects and run unit tests.

FAKE is built in F# and the scripts you use to create the automated build process are also created in F#. I've used FAKE in projects such as FsUnit and found it to be very helpful! It's also a great way to get F# "in the door" for any groups or organizations that may be hesitant about bringing in F#. You can find several examples for getting started with FAKE here (*https://github.com/fsharp/FAKE/tree/develop/Samples*).

FAKE leverages MSBuild, so in addition to the power of F# and the various custom plug-ins that FAKE provides, you can take advantage of everything that MSBuild has to offer.

NuGet

I've talked about NuGet at multiple points throughout the book; however, I haven't provided much information about how to use NuGet. If NuGet is new to you, the best way to get started with it is to visit the NuGet website (*http://nuget.org/*) and read the documentation. A high-level overview is also provided in the next section.

Basic Usage

There are two primary ways to use NuGet from Visual Studio. One is through the Package Manager Console. Another is through the Manage NuGet Packages UI. Throughout this book I often mention that you can install a specific package with the provided package ID. Once you have that ID, it's very easy to install the package into the desired project using the Package Manager Console.

You may be wondering where to find the Package Manager Console. One way to get to it is through Edit→Other Windows→Package Manager Console. Another way is through Tools→Library Package Manager→Package Manager Console. Both options will result in opening the Package Manager Console.

After launching the Package Manager Console, you will see a window that looks like Figure A-1.

Figure A-1. NuGet Package Manager Console

You can then select the desired target project via the drop down labeled "Default project" and type a command such as the following to install a package:

```
Install-package packageID
```

The Manage NuGet Packages UI approach is also very easy. Simply right-click on References in the desired target project and select Manage NuGet Packages. You can then search for the desired package and install it. Figure A-2 shows the Manage NuGet Packages screen.

Figure A-2. Manage NuGet Packages screen

Useful NuGet Packages

I've pointed out a number of useful NuGet packages throughout the book. The following list includes several others in which you might be interested (the descriptions of these packages come directly from NuGet):

PDFsharp *(by PDFsharp-Team)*
> PDFsharp is the Open Source .NET library that easily creates and processes PDF documents on the fly from any .NET language. The same drawing routines can be used to create PDF documents, draw on the screen, or send output to any printer. This is PDFsharp based on GDI+.

FSharpx.Core *(by mausch danmohl sforkmann panesofglass)*
> FSharpx is a library for the .NET platform implementing general functional constructs on top of the F# core library. Its main target is F# but it aims to be compatible with all .NET languages wherever possible. It currently implements:
>
> - Several standard monads: State, Reader, Writer, Either, Continuation, Distribution
> - Iteratee
> - Validation app, and more

FSPowerPack.Community *(by danmohl)*

The F# PowerPack is a collection of libraries and tools for use with the F# programming languages provided by the F# team at Microsoft.

PicoMvc *(by robertpi)*

A thin veneer of F#ness around several different frameworks to make a lightweight MVC framework.

FSharp.Testing *(by sforkmann)*

Some extensions that help to make F# code testable from C# test projects.

FSharpx.Observable *(by sforkmann)*

FSharpx is a library for the .NET platform implementing general functional constructs on top of the F# core library. Its main target is F# but it aims to be compatible with all .NET languages wherever possible. This library implements a mini-Reactive Extensions (MiniRx) and was authored by Phil Trelford.

FSharpx.Http *(by sforkmann)*

FSharpx is a library for the .NET platform implementing general functional constructs on top of the F# core library. Its main target is F# but it aims to be compatible with all .NET languages wherever possible. This library provides common features for working with HTTP applications.

Soma *(by taedium)*

Soma is an O/R mapping framework developed in F#. Soma supports not only F#, but also C# and VB.NET.

Math.NET Numerics F# Modules (by mathnet cdrnet)

F# Modules for Math.NET Numerics, the numerical foundation of the Math.NET project, aims to provide methods and algorithms for numerical computations in science, engineering, and everyday use. Numerics is the result of merging dnAnalytics with Math.NET Iridium and is intended to replace both.

FParsec *(by panesofglass huwman Khanage)*

FParsec is a parser combinator library for F#.

FSharpChart *(by carl nolan)*

FSharpChart contains F#-friendly wrappers for the types in the System.Win dows.Forms.DataVisualization.Charting namespace (*http://msdn.micro soft.com/en-us/library/system.windows.forms.datavisualization.charting.aspx*), which makes it easy to interactively chart data from F# Interactive.

Math.NET Numerics F# Module Code Samples (by mathnet cdrnet)

This package contains samples that demonstrate the use of the F# Modules for the Math.NET Numerics library. Math.NET Numerics is the numerical foundation of the Math.NET project, aiming to provide methods and algorithms for numerical computations in science, engineering, and everyday use.

`FsRavenDbTools` *(by robertpi)*

Help using RavenDB from F# (and Newtonsoft.Json).

`FsLinqFixed` *(by robertpi)*

This is the F# `PowerPack.Linq` library, based on the F# PowerPack code drop under the OSS approved Apache 2.0 license from here (*http://fsharppowerpack.code plex.com/*).

`Fracture` *(by panesofglass)*

`Fracture` is an F#-based socket implementation for high-speed, high-throughput applications. It is built on top of `SocketAsyncEventArgs`, which minimizes the memory fragmentation common in the IAsyncResult pattern.

KinkumaFramework F# (F# MVVM Framework; by okazuki)

Prism-based F# MVVM Framework.

`FSPowerPack.Parallel.Seq.Community` *(by danmohl)*

This package includes `FSPowerPack.Core.Community` as well as the `Parallel .Seq` libraries. The F# PowerPack is a collection of libraries and tools for use with the F# programming languages provided by the F# team at Microsoft.

`log4f` *(by robertpi)*

A thin veneer of F#ness around `log4net`.

`FSPowerPack.Community.Sample` *(by danmohl)*

This package includes the entire F# PowerPack plus a simple sample on how to use it. The F# PowerPack is a collection of libraries and tools for use with the F# programming languages provided by the F# team at Microsoft.

`FSharpEnt.Common` *(by colinbul)*

Common. F# extensions for the enterprise; this now encompasses `FSharpEnt .Json`, `FSharpEnt.Etl`, and `FSharpEnt.Actors`.

`Focco` *(by panesofglass)*

`Focco` is a quick-and-dirty, literate-programming-style documentation generator.

`FSPowerPack.Metadata.Community` *(by danmohl)*

This package includes `FSPowerPack.Core.Community` as well as the `Metadata` libraries. The F# PowerPack is a collection of libraries and tools for use with the F# programming languages provided by the F# team at Microsoft.

`FSharpEnt.RabbitMq` *(by colinbul)*

F# RabbitMq client wrapper.

`Samples.WindowsAzure.Marketplace` *(by dsyme)*

Sample. F# 3.0 Type Provider giving access to data sets here (*datamarket.azure.com*).

`FSharp.Reactive` *2.0.120725-rc (by sforkmann panesofglass)*
An F#-friendly wrapper for the Reactive Extensions.

ExpectThat

ExpectThat is an assertion library that can be helpful when testing LiveScript, Coffee-Script, and/or JavaScript. The syntax of ExpectThat is heavily influenced by FsUnit and as such I have chosen to include it in this appendix. As with FsUnit, there are several flavors of ExpectThat that correspond to your favorite JavaScript testing framework. Currently, options include support for QUnit, Jasmine, Mocha, and Pavlov. ExpectThat also works in both the browser and Node.js. You can find the source for ExpectThat as well as several examples here (*https://github.com/dmohl/expectThat*).

The easiest way to get started with ExpectThat in Visual Studio is to do the following:

1. Install the Mindscape Web Workbench (available on Visual Studio Gallery (*http://bit.ly/mindscape-workbench*)).

2. Create a web project from any desired project template.

3. Install one of the ExpectThat NuGet packages such as `ExpectThat.Mocha`.

4. Save the *example.spec.coffee* file so that the underlying JavaScript file is generated. This file can be found in the *Scripts\Specs* folder of the web project that was created in step 2.

5. Open the *Index.html* file in your favorite browser.

The CoffeeScript code used in the *example.spec.coffee* file is as follows and the output of running these specs is shown in Figure A-3 (I'll talk more about CoffeeScript in Appendix C):

```
describe "Example Mocha Specifications", ->
    foo = "bar"
    describe "When testing should equal", ->
        expectThat -> foo.should equal "bar"
    describe "When testing shouldnt equal", ->
        expectThat -> foo.shouldnt equal "baz"
    describe "When testing for true", ->
        expectThat -> (foo is "bar").should be true
        expectThat -> (foo is "baz").shouldnt be true
    describe "When testing for false", ->
        expectThat -> (foo is "baz").should be false
        expectThat -> (foo is "bar").shouldnt be false
    describe "When testing to and be", ->
        expectThat -> foo.should be equal to "bar"
        expectThat -> foo.shouldnt be equal to "bah"
    describe "When testing for null or undefined", ->
        testNull = null
        testUndefined = undefined
```

```
            expectThat -> (testNull is null).should be true
            expectThat -> (testNull isnt null).shouldnt be true
            expectThat -> (testUndefined is undefined).should be true
            expectThat -> (testUndefined is undefined).shouldnt be false
        describe "When testing for throw", ->
            expectThat -> (-> throw "test exception").should throwException
            expectThat ->
                (-> throw "test exception").should throwException "test exception"
        describe "When testing for greater than", ->
            expectThat -> 10.should be greaterThan 9
            expectThat -> 9.1.shouldnt be greaterThan 10
        describe "When testing for less than", ->
            expectThat -> 10.should be lessThan 11
            expectThat -> 10.1.shouldnt be lessThan 10
```

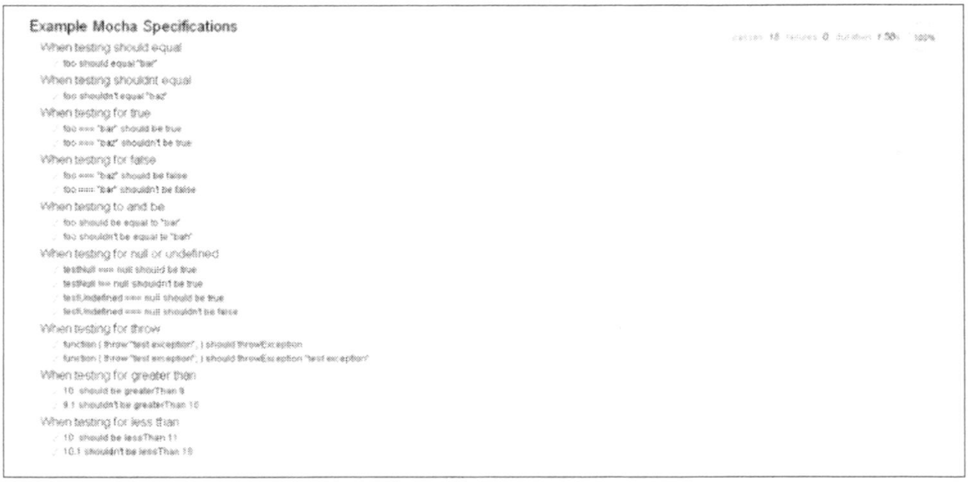

Figure A-3. Example of running Mocha with ExpectThat

Useful Websites

This appendix points out a few websites that can be very helpful when creating F# web, cloud, and mobile solutions. A few of the sites have been referenced periodically throughout this book. All provide excellent resources for learning more about F# and/or various web development libraries.

fssnip.net

The fssnip.net website (*http://fssnip.net/*) is an excellent provider of F# examples. The site was built by Tomas Petricek with the intent of providing a mechanism for F# developers to share targeted snippets of code with other F# developers. The About page of the site indicates that fssnip.net "is similar to other Pastebin services, but focuses only on F#."

The site currently includes snippets that target everything from web to gaming to DSLs and the list is growing daily. This makes it a great resource if you are ever trying to find an example of how to accomplish a specific task. You can also easily submit your own snippets.

tryfsharp.org

The tryfsharp.org site (*http://www.tryfsharp.org*) provides an excellent tutorial for those just getting started with F#. Additionally, and perhaps more importantly, it also provides an online REPL that allows experimentation with the language without requiring any setup. This makes it very easy to try out F# when you haven't yet downloaded the associated compiler and/or don't have it on the particular computer at which you are currently working.

Visual Studio Gallery

I've referenced Visual Studio Gallery many times throughout this book. It is through Visual Studio Gallery that many of the templates and tools I have described are distributed. In addition to the handful of templates I've gone over in detail, Visual Studio Gallery contains a large number of other useful F#-related Visual Studio extensions.

The easiest way to find extensions related to F# is to visit the Visual Studio Gallery website (*http://visualstudiogallery.msdn.microsoft.com*) and search for "F#" or "fsharp". You can then select a specific category such as Tools, Controls, or Templates to narrow the results. I strongly encourage you to see what is out there and to take advantage of the various works provided by the community.

jQueryMobile.com

Throughout this book, I have mentioned jQuery Mobile many times in the form of various examples. If you haven't had a chance to check out jQuery Mobile, I strongly encourage you to peruse the online Docs (*http://jquerymobile.com/*). You can also download both the core files for the library as well as the source (*https://github.com/jquery/jquery-mobile*) for the jQueryMobile.com site.

Client-Side Technologies That Go Well with F#

In the last chapter of this book, I showed you a few options for creating web-centric, client-side code in a functional style. In this appendix I'll introduce a few other client-side technologies that go well with F#. While this introduction does not comprehensively cover any of the technologies, it will give you enough information to get started.

CoffeeScript

I've mentioned CoffeeScript a few times throughout this book. CoffeeScript is similar to LiveScript in that it's a unique language that compiles to JavaScript. As I mentioned in Chapter 5, it is one of the parents of LiveScript, therefore much of what I stated about LiveScript also applies to CoffeeScript. The biggest difference between LiveScript and CoffeeScript is that LiveScript has more of a focus on providing support for developing in a more functional style.

 While this appendix focuses on client-side technologies, CoffeeScript is not limited to only client-side development. It can also be used for server-side development thanks to Node.js.

You may be wondering why you might wish to choose CoffeeScript over LiveScript. CoffeeScript has been steadily growing in popularity. Because of this, it has a great support group, lots of online examples, and a growing subset of tool support. The biggest things you lose when choosing CoffeeScript over LiveScript include several of the functional stylistic concepts that LiveScript provides as well as a few of the niceties of Coco, which as I said in Chapter 5 is one of the parents of LiveScript.

The easiest way to write CoffeeScript within Visual Studio is to install a Visual Studio extension called the Mindscape Web Workbench (*http://visualstudiogallery.msdn.micro soft.com/2b96d16a-c986-4501-8f97-8008f9db141a*) from Visual Studio Gallery. This free extension provides integrated support for Visual Studio 2010 and Visual Studio 2012 that makes it very simple to write CoffeeScript.

Let's quickly walk through an example. You may recall the simple sample provided for LiveScript in Chapter 5 that checked to see whether a provided day was part of the weekend. Here's the LiveScript code to refresh your memory:

```
weekend = <[ sat sun ]>

isWeekend = (dayOfWeek) ->
    | dayOfWeek in weekend => true
    | _ => false

'sun' |> isWeekend |> console.log
```

To create this same example in CoffeeScript using the Mindscape Web Workbench we do the following:

1. Install the Mindscape Web Workbench Visual Studio extension (if not already done).

2. Add a CoffeeScript item to any desired web project and name it appropriately.

3. In the resultant *.coffee* file, add the following code:

```
weekend = ["sat", "sun"]

isWeekend = (dayOfWeek) ->
    dayOfWeek in weekend

console.log isWeekend "sun"
```

That's all there is to it. The Mindscape Web Workbench extension will automatically take care of compiling the syntax you write in the *.coffee* file and place the output in a *.js* file with the same name. You can then reference this *.js* file in your web solution just as you would any other *.js* file.

Sass

Sass is a tool that falls into the category of a CSS preprocessor language. CSS preprocessor languages allow you to more easily write reusable, maintainable, and flexible CSS. They accomplish this by providing a syntax that allows you to be more expressive with the creation of your CSS, and then they convert that syntax into the plain old CSS that you would have normally written. In addition to making your CSS more readable and maintainable, another reason to use Sass in your F# web projects is because of the option for the use of significant whitespace rather than braces.

 Sass is not the only CSS preprocessor language option. Other popular options include LESS and Stylus. In the interest of space, I have chosen to focus only on Sass; however, I encourage you to also check out other options to determine which is best for you.

Let's see it in action. In the LiveScript To Do application example I showed in Chapter 5, a file named *Site.css* (*http://bit.ly/SYCZrP*) was used to add styles. The file contains the following CSS:

```
.detail {
    margin: 10px 0px;
}

.column-header {
    padding-bottom: 5px;
    margin: 5px 0;
    border-bottom: 1px solid #EEE;
}

.draggable {
    height: 50px;
    -webkit-border-radius: 4px;
    -moz-border-radius: 4px;
    border-radius: 4px;
    -webkit-box-shadow: inset 0 1px 1px rgba(0, 0, 0, 0.05);
    -moz-box-shadow: inset 0 1px 1px rgba(0,0,0,0.05);
    box-shadow: inset 0 1px 1px rgba(0, 0, 0, 0.05);
    margin-bottom: 10px;
    padding: 10px;
    vertical-align:middle;
}

.tasks {
    min-height: 100px;
}
```

This is fairly typical CSS, but it would be nice if there was a way to remove some of the duplicity associated with having to support multiple browsers as well as to remove characters that don't add value, such as the braces and semicolons. I can do both of these things and much more with Sass. The following shows the syntax used to accomplish these goals:

```
@mixin border-radius($pxl)
    -webkit-border-radius: $pxl
    -moz-border-radius: $pxl
    border-radius: $pxl

@mixin box-shadow($val)
    -webkit-box-shadow: $val
    -moz-box-shadow: $val
    box-shadow: $val

.detail
    margin: 10px 0px

.column-header
    padding-bottom: 5px
    margin: 5px 0
    border-bottom: 1px solid #EEE

.draggable
    height: 50px
    @include border-radius(4px)
    @include box-shadow(inset 0 1px 1px rgba(0, 0, 0, 0.05))
    margin-bottom: 10px
    padding: 10px
    vertical-align: middle

.tasks
    min-height: 100px
```

This example only begins to show the power of Sass. Additional features include the ability to create and use variables, the ability to include operators and functions in your CSS, and niceties such as string interpolation. You can find more information on the Sass website (*http://sass-lang.com/*).

Underscore.js

In Chapter 5, I briefly pointed out a library named `prelude.ls` that provides a number of functions that allow you to write web-centric, client-side code with a more functional style. `Underscore.js` was written by the same person who created CoffeeScript and it has a similar goal as `prelude.ls`, but with more features (not all of which are specifically targeted at a functional style).

The Underscore.js site (*http://underscorejs.org/*) contains a large number of examples, so I will only provide a quick, high-level list of features:

- Collection-related functions include `map`, `reduce`, `filter`, `all`, `any`, `sortBy`, and `groupBy`.

- Array-related functions include `first`, `last`, `union`, `intersect`, `flatten`, and `zip`.

- Helper functions include `bind`, `memoize`, `throttle`, and `once`.
- Object-related functions include `isString`, `isDate`, `isBoolean`, `has`, `clone`, and `tap`.
- Other great features include a templating engine and chaining.

 This is far from a complete list of functions and/or features that `Underscore.js` provides. I strongly recommend that you visit the Underscore.js site (*http://underscorejs.org/*) for more information.

Index

Symbols

A

We'd like to hear your suggestions for improving our indexes. Send email to index@oreilly.com.

About the Author

Daniel Mohl is a Microsoft F# MVP, F# and C# Insider, blogger, speaker, and event organizer. He has a blog (*http://blog.danielmohl.com*) and you can follow him on Twitter (*http://twitter.com/dmohl*).

Colophon

The animal on the cover of *Building Web, Cloud, and Mobile Solutions with F#* is a Barbel flyingfish (*Exocoetus monocirrhus*). This fish is distributed throughout the Indo-Pacific and Eastern Pacific regions and widespread in the tropical zone at a depth of 0 to 20 meters. Its maximum length is 23 centimeters and its body is brown along the top and silver below.

This fish has an elongated, broadly cylindrical body with a short head and a blunt snout. Its mouth is small and the lower jaw is slightly longer than the upper one, with no teeth. Its fins have no spines and its tail is deeply forked with a longer lower lobe. Its scales are large, smooth, and easily shed.

This fish is known to leap out of the water and glide for considerable distances above the surface. Its diet consists of zooplankton, crustacean, fish larvae, and fish eggs. Its migration is cyclical and predictable and covers more than 100 kilometers.

The cover image is from *Johnson's Natural History*. The cover font is Adobe ITC Garamond. The text font is Adobe Minion Pro; the heading font is Adobe Myriad Condensed; and the code font is Dalton Maag's Ubuntu Mono.

Have it your way.

Get even more for your money.

Join the O'Reilly Community, and register the O'Reilly books you own. It's free, and you'll get:

- $4.99 ebook upgrade offer
- 40% upgrade offer on O'Reilly print books
- Membership discounts on books and events
- Free lifetime updates to ebooks and videos
- Multiple ebook formats, DRM FREE
- Participation in the O'Reilly community
- Newsletters
- Account management
- 100% Satisfaction Guarantee

Signing up is easy:

1. **Go to: oreilly.com/go/register**
2. **Create an O'Reilly login.**
3. **Provide your address.**
4. **Register your books.**

Note: English-language books only

To order books online:
oreilly.com/store

For questions about products or an order:
orders@oreilly.com

To sign up to get topic-specific email announcements and/or news about upcoming books, conferences, special offers, and new technologies:
elists@oreilly.com

For technical questions about book content:
booktech@oreilly.com

To submit new book proposals to our editors:
proposals@oreilly.com

O'Reilly books are available in multiple DRM-free ebook formats. For more information:
oreilly.com/ebooks

O'REILLY®

Spreading the knowledge of innovators | oreilly.com

FEB 0 8 2013

9 781449 333768